Buller's Professional Course in
BARTENDING

Buller's
Professional Course
in
BARTENDING
for Home Study

by Jon Buller

THE HARVARD COMMON PRESS

HARVARD AND BOSTON, MASSACHUSETTS

The Harvard Common Press
535 Albany Street
Boston, Massachusetts 02118

Library of Congress Cataloging in Publication Data
Buller, Jon, 1943–
   Buller's Professional course in bartending for home study.

   Includes index.
   1. Bartending.   I. Title
TX951.B795   1983   647'.95   82-23309
ISBN 0-916782-34-4
ISBN 0-916782-33-6 (pbk.)

Cover and illustrations by Jon Buller
Back cover photograph by Jeremy Dodd

10   9   8   7   6   5   4   3   2   1

Contents

Introduction

I F YOU READ this book carefully and memorize how to
prepare the thirty basic cocktails, you should know
enough about bartending to start work in almost any bar in
America and many abroad.

Most other bartending books are primarily collections
of recipes for mixed drinks. They may be useful for
reference, but they can actually be confusing to someone
who would like to learn the craft of commercial bartending.
Many of the drinks are obscure, obsolete, or popular only
in a very limited region; and the great quantity of recipes
can be bewildering to the beginning bartender. Discussion
of the actual *techniques* of professional bartending in these
books ranges from the inadequate to the nonexistent.

This book's professional course in bartending gives the
same information that you would learn from a good

bartending school. There is an appendix of recipes, but in the main text the emphasis is on the few dozen basic drinks that make up 99 percent of the orders in American bars. You learn not only the recipe but the correct technique for preparing each drink, whether it be a stir drink, a shake drink, or a build drink. There are also chapters on handling multiple orders, on free pouring and measured pouring, on customer relations and tips, and on every aspect of professional bartending. Here is everything you need to know in order to start pouring drinks for a living, to make drinks in your home bar as they are made professionally, or simply to satisfy an armchair interest in that unique American contribution to world culture, the art of mixology.

1. Welcome to the Club

THOREAU SAID that he did not want to feel, when it came time for him to die, that he had not lived. Whatever the drawbacks of bartending, this is not one of them. As a bartender, you are surrounded by talk, laughter, music, and passion. Occasionally—just often enough to make it interesting—there are also tears and anger; but, in general, people go to bars to enjoy themselves.

What are the qualities of a good bartender? A good sense of humor always helps in dealing with people. A little patience is essential. You need a neat, pleasant appearance. You need a little sense of diplomacy, a little manual and mental dexterity, and clean fingernails. You need to be orderly, and often you need to be quick. You need to be able to work standing up for eight hours at a time. You need to be at least eighteen, and possibly twenty-one, depending on state laws.

"Sherry cobbler" is indeed a most excellent drink. I was taught to make it when I was an undergraduate by no less a person that the late "Father" Stanton, who was as good a fellow as he was a godly man; and the preliminary process of "cataracting" the wine and the ice and the lemon from two properly handled and not pusillanimously approximated soda-water tumblers is a beautiful and noble occupation.

—GEORGE SAINTSBURY

In a way, bartending is an easy job. After a little practice almost anyone can pour a scotch on the rocks, empty an ashtray, and make change. And there is a kind of satisfaction in that—the satisfaction of performing simple tasks well. At the same time, bartending is a job that allows room for real excellence. There are people who can legitimately be called great bartenders, something you cannot say about every job. A great bartender develops a multilevel mind. One level deals with the practical necessities of the job, and this calls for close attention to a multitude of small details. Another level deals with customers on a personal level, and helps foster in the bar an atmosphere of friendliness, comfort, and refuge. After a little practice, handling this counterpoint can be a lot of fun.

On the negative side, there is the problem of dealing with the occasional rude drunk, a problem that every bartender faces from time to time. This is always unpleasant, but, like everything else, you get better at it with practice. Chapter 19 of this book deals with this matter separately.

As for money, the pay ranges in 1983 from $3.50 to $6.75 an hour, and the tips range anywhere from 50 percent of your pay to 200 percent. A small number of bartenders go off this scale at one end or the other. On the low end, there are some "service" bartenders (that is, those bartenders who have no contact with the public, and make drinks solely to be served by waiters and waitresses) who make no tips at all. On the high side, there are some bars, often in places like New York and Las Vegas, where the bartenders can consistently pull in $200 a night in tips.

Obviously, there are jobs offering more prestige and more money. Yet for certain people in certain situations, bartending can be the perfect employment. The work place is less dirty, noisy, and dangerous than the average factory. The training you need can be acquired relatively quickly. It can be a good job for students, because in many areas hiring greatly increases in the summer or winter tourist season, coinciding with school vacations. For young people in particular, a stretch as a bartender can be a kind of education in itself—a chance to communicate with all kinds of people.

Bartending has traditionally been popular with people in the arts and with other self-employed individuals who need a supplemental job. Such people often work part time at night, in order to have the days available for their regular work. With a little practice, bartending is easily put out of your mind when you are off, leaving you free for whatever it is you want to do when you are not a bartender. And it is a skill that travels well. Wherever liquor is legal, there are usually bars.

Increasingly, also, people with completely adequate incomes will take a bartending job one or two nights a week almost as a form of recreation. If their regular work is sedentary, tending bar will give them several hours of continuous activity. And if their regular work is intellectually demanding and solitary, they may enjoy the change to a kind of activity that is, by comparison, fairly simple and pleasantly sociable.

No one really comes to know Everyman better than the bartender. You will see couples on their first date together, divorced people, and old people who are widowed. People just off the train will ask you, "Say, what goes on in this town, anyway?" And others will tell you they lived here thirty years ago, and how the town has changed.

As a bartender I especially enjoy the impromptu discussions that occur in a bar full of total strangers, all slightly lubricated. One of the great things about bars is that you can go in and start talking to total strangers about what is wrong with modern medicine and the Red Sox and your boss, and instead of edging away—as they would in a laundromat, or library, or supermarket—people will respond.

From time to time, customers come into the bar where I work and say, "You know, I used to be a bartender . . ." Almost always this is said in a tone that lets you know they remember the job fondly. If it is not too busy, we talk shop for a few minutes. Many of these ex-bartenders have moved on to higher-paying professions, and certainly have no thoughts of getting back in the business. But I honestly cannot think of any who gave me the feeling that they looked back on their period of tending bar with regret, and most of them have a funny story or two to tell from the time when they were on the other side of the stick.

Basic Tools

liquor bottles with pourers • mixing glass and spoon • shaker cap • strainer • shot glass • bar mop • ice

2. Tools of the Trade

I F YOU ARE FORTUNATE enough to get a learn-on-the-job position, the tools will come with the job.

If you want to use this book as a home-study school, however, you will probably want to get a basic set of bartending tools and glassware, and spend a few evenings practicing the homework assignments in Chapters 3 through 10. This should be enough hands-on practice for you to be able to get away with saying that you have had some experience as a bartender. Often this makes the difference in getting a job. (More on this in Chapter 26.)

A basic set of tools should not be expensive. They are sold by restaurant suppliers, found in the yellow pages under "Restaurant Equipment and Supplies," and some-times also in department and liquor stores. Later, these tools can be used at your home bar, and for working private parties. Here is what you will need:

Practice bottles. A half dozen or so empty liquor bottles, preferably of different colors, are all that is needed. It is not necessary to have a different bottle for every liquor mentioned in the book. Just let the clear bottles stand for all the clear liquors (vodka, gin), the brown bottles for the dark liquors (whiskey, cognac), and the green bottles for the cordials. For practice, the bottles should be filled with water, not booze.

Pourers. The cheap kind work just as well as the pseudo-chromes.

Shaker cap and strainer. In a commercial bar you will have several different sizes of shaker caps, each to fit a different size glass, but for practice you should be able to get by with just the large size.

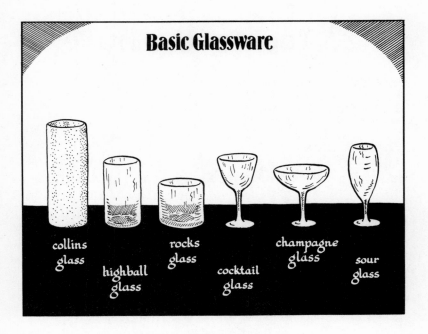

Basic Glassware

collins glass   highball glass   rocks glass   cocktail glass   champagne glass   sour glass

Shot glass. These also come in various sizes. For learning, the best size is one ounce, with a line marking ½ ounce.

Ice. Buy a few pounds. Even allowing for recycling, you are not going to get much practicing done with two trays from your refrigerator.

Barmop. A slightly damp cloth will serve.

Glassware. Pictured above are the six basic glasses used to serve mixed drinks. There are also special glasses for serving certain straight drinks, such as the wine glass, the brandy snifter, and the cordial pony. These will be mentioned in later chapters. In addition, many bars use novelty glasses for certain drinks—large tulip glasses for Bloody Marys, skull mugs for Zombies, or whatever. For practice all you really need is a few each of the rocks glasses, highball glasses, and cocktail glasses.

3. Free Pouring: "One . . . Two . . . Three . . . *Hup!*"

A PROFESSIONAL BARTENDER should be able to pour an ounce (or half an ounce, or two ounces) accurately and consistently without using a shot glass. This is a skill that can be learned by the following method:

Fill an empty liquor bottle with water and put in a pourer. To pour an ounce, invert the bottle completely over a shaker cap and count to yourself in four even beats:

"One . . . two . . . three . . . *hup!* "

At *"hup!"* the bottle is quickly righted, with a slight twist of the wrist that prevents spillage. Note that the bottle is held completely upside down. This gives a quicker, more uniform flow.

Now pour the water from the shaker cap into the one-ounce shot glass. If there is less than an ounce, you

counted too fast; if more, you counted too slowly. Try again, adjusting your counting speed accordingly. Continue practicing until you can free-pour an ounce four times out of five with an error of no more than a few drops.

HOMEWORK: Once you can pour an ounce, practice pouring a half ounce, an ounce and a half, and two ounces with the following counts:

½ oz. — One . . . two . . . *hup!*
1 oz. — One . . . two . . . three . . . *hup!*
1½ oz. — One . . . two . . . three . . . four . . . five . . . *hup!*
2 oz. — One . . . two . . . three . . . four . . . five . . . six . . . *hup!*

Practice pouring with your right hand, your left hand, and finally with both hands at once. You will find later that the count must be slowed somewhat for the syrupy liquors, like Kahlua.

Counting is a crutch to get you started. After you have been working for a while, you will be able to estimate amounts correctly without counting.

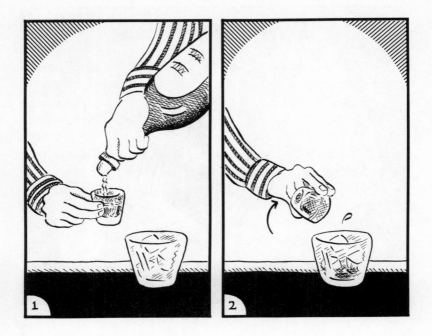

4. Measured Pouring

S OME BARS REQUIRE their bartenders to use a shot glass to measure all their drinks. Others require only new bartenders to use the shot glass during their break-in period.

A shot glass used for measuring should be held so that its rim is right next to, but slightly higher than, the glass that the drink will be served in. The other hand pours the liquor, either to the line marked on the glass, or to the brim, or halfway in between—this depends on the policy of the individual bar. Then the shot is quickly tipped into the serving glass. While the shot glass is still in your hand, dip it into the clear sink to rinse it.

Measured pouring is used primarily in very large establishments, and in places where management likes to keep very strict control on the amount of liquor used.

Bartenders generally do not like using the shot glass. It slows you down, and it seems to take away some part of your professionalism. It also removes the possibility of "pouring a good drink" for a regular customer. This can be an important part of your relationship with your regulars, and, if it is not overdone, it can be good for your boss's business as well as for your tips. It is also helpful to have the option of occasionally pouring a weak drink.

The advantages of measured pouring versus free pouring will be discussed further in Chapter 25, Bar Management.

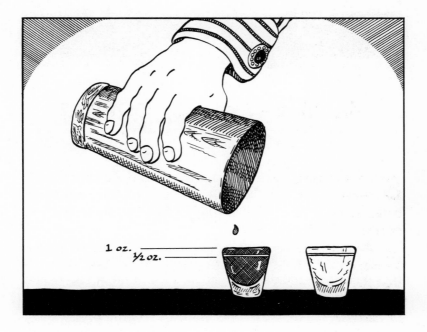

5. Stir Drinks

I N ADDITION to serving drinks, a bartender also provides a touch of ceremony. Perhaps the most essential ceremony is the preparation of the stir drink, such as the Martini.

When a customer orders a Martini, a Manhattan, or any of the other stir drinks, always ask if he or she would like it *straight up* (without ice) or *on the rocks* (with). If *on the rocks*, the ingredients are poured directly into a rocks glass filled with ice, and served with a stirrer. For drinks served *up*, the ingredients are stirred with ice in a shaker glass, and then strained into another glass, generally a cocktail glass. The result is a drink which is chilled in the making, but which does not get diluted by melting ice. To illustrate this procedure we will use the Martini.

Dry Martini

2 ounces gin
½ ounce dry vermouth
GLASS: cocktail
FRUIT: olive

Put a scoop of ice—or a handful of ice, if you are practicing at home, and don't have a scoop—into the large mixing glass, counting

"One . . . two . . . *hup*! . . . four . . . five . . . six . . . *hup*!"

At the first "*hup*!" stop pouring the vermouth. Continue pouring the gin until the second "*hup*!"

Stir 1½ times with the mixing spoon, and dip the spoon in the clear sink (see Chapter 17) to rinse. Put the strainer on the large mixing glass and pour the Martini into a cocktail glass, always pouring over the prongs of the strainer. Rinse strainer.

The Martini

"Professor" Jerry Thomas was the father of American mixology. He tended bar in San Francisco in the middle of the nineteenth century, and wrote a book called The Bon Vivants Companion, or, How to Mix Drinks. *One morning a man named Martinez asked him for a hangover remedy. In a flash of inspiration Professor Thomas mixed together:*

1 dash bitters
2 dashes maraschino liqueur
1 shot Old Tom Gin (a sweet gin)
1 wineglass sweet vermouth
2 lumps ice
2 dashes sugar syrup
Shake; add slice of lemon.

This became known as a Martinez Cocktail. The drink eventually made its way to the East Coast, where, in the early years of this century, a bartender named Martini di Arma Taggia at the Knickerbocker Hotel in New York created the Dry Martini. He simplified Thomas's original recipe, used dry vermouth instead of sweet, and changed the name slightly, making it Italian rather than Spanish. Like modern architecture, the modern Martini does away with all but the essentials: gin, and dry vermouth. And there are those who question the need for the vermouth.

If your drink is a little short—and it is always better to be a little short than a little over—pour a splash of gin into the mixing glass, swirl it around with the ice, and bring the drink up to the proper level.

The glass itself should also be chilled. If Martini glasses are not kept in a cooler, they may be placed rim downwards in the ice tray while the drinks are being mixed.

The other stir drinks are made with the same basic

procedure, using different ingredients in different amounts. When ordered *up* they are always served in a cocktail glass.

Manhattan

2 ounces whiskey
½ ounce sweet vermouth
GLASS: cocktail
FRUIT: cherry

Vodka Gimlet

2 ounces vodka
½ ounce Rose's Lime Juice
GLASS: cocktail
FRUIT: lime wedge

Stinger

1½ ounces brandy
1 ounce white crème de menthe
GLASS: cocktail

Cocktail glasses vary in size from bar to bar. The above recipes are based on a 2½-ounce glass, which is about average. The amount poured in rocks drinks can also vary from bar to bar, depending on the size of the glass, the size of the ice cubes, and how close to the brim the drink is poured. Usually a bar will pour less in their rocks drinks than their up drinks. The pouring policies of a bar are usually explained to you when you start working, but sometimes you have to look around and discover them for yourself.

COROLLARY DRINKS

Extra Dry Martini. Use only a few drops of vermouth.

Bone Dry Martini. Use straight gin.

Gibson. A Martini that is garnished with a cocktail onion instead of an olive.

Manhattan (West Coast version). Use bourbon instead of whiskey.

Dry Manhattan. Use dry vermouth instead of sweet, lemon twist instead of cherry.

Perfect Manhattan. Use half dry vermouth, half sweet vermouth, twist instead of cherry.

Rob Roy. Like a Manhattan, but use scotch instead of whiskey.

Gin Gimlet. Use gin instead of vodka.

HOMEWORK: Make five each of the four basic stir drinks. Repeat, this time working for speed. Memorize the recipes, and the corollary drinks.

6. Shake Drinks

THE REASON DRINKS are shaken is to blend ingredients that would otherwise remain separate. A secondary reason is to put a foamy head on the drink.

Milk and cream drinks always need to be shaken, except for those drinks that call for a spoonful of milk or cream to be floated on top of the drink. The other ingredients that always indicate a shake drink are lemon juice—or lemon mix—and lime juice.

To illustrate the shake drink, we will use the Whiskey Sour:

Whiskey Sour

1½ ounces whiskey
1 ounce lemon mix
GLASS: sour glass
FRUIT: orange and cherry

17

The whiskey (one, two, three, four, five, *hup!*) and the lemon mix and ice are poured into a large mixing glass, just as if one were making a stir drink. The lemon mix in the bar where you work may come out of the soda-gun system, in which case you will have to judge the amount by eye, rather than by counting. The shaker cap is then placed on top of the mixing glass, and the drink is given four or five vigorous shakes (see illustration). The direction of the shake should be parallel to the bar, and not directed at the customers. Then the shaker cap is removed—sometimes it gets stuck and it needs a little sideways tap to free it—and a strainer is placed on the mixing glass, and the drink is poured into a chilled sour glass. Add fruit and serve.

The above procedure is used for making shake drinks that are ordered *straight up.* For drinks ordered *on the rocks,* the same ingredients are poured directly into a rocks glass. A smaller shaker is used that fits the rocks glass, and the drink is shaken right in the glass in which it will be served. Remove shaker cap, add fruit and stirrer, and serve.

The Tom Collins

The Tom Collins took its surname from John Collins, a headwaiter who developed the drink at Limmer's Hotel in London, during the Regency period at the beginning of the nineteenth century. The drink took its first name from Old Tom Gin, a sweet gin that was the basic ingredient. Today the Tom Collins is made with dry gin. The John Collins is a variation that is made with whiskey instead of gin. A poem from the Regency survives that remembers Mr. Collins:

My name is John Collins, head waiter at Limmer's,
Corner of Conduit Street, Hanover Square.
My chief occupation is filling the brimmers
For all the young gentlemen frequenters there.

Although the Whiskey Sour is most common, sours can be made with almost any liquor. You will have calls for Vodka Sours, Scotch Sours, Apricot Brandy Sours, and so on. When ordered *up*, they are always served in a sour glass. All sours are garnished with an orange and a cherry.

Daiquiri

1½ ounces rum
1 ounce lime mix
GLASS: cocktail
FRUIT: lime wedge

Margarita

1 ounce tequila
½ ounce triple sec
1 ounce lime mix
GLASS: cocktail, with salted rim
FRUIT: lime wedge

Brandy Alexander

¾ ounce brandy
¾ ounce dark crème de cacao
1 ounce cream (or milk)
GLASS: champagne
GARNISH: nutmeg

Grasshopper

¾ ounce green crème de menthe
¾ ounce white crème de cacao
1 ounce cream (or milk)
GLASS: champagne

The rest of the drinks in this chapter are always served as tall drinks with ice—never straight up—and are shaken in their glasses.

Bloody Mary

1½ ounces vodka
½ ounce lime juice
4 dashes worcestershire sauce
1 dash tabasco
Salt and pepper
Tomato juice to fill glass; then shake
GLASS: Collins glass with ice
FRUIT: celery stalk

This is a standard recipe for a scratch Bloody Mary. It only needs to be shaken once or twice gently. In bars that use prepared Bloody Mary mix, no shaking is needed at all. Just add vodka and serve.

Tom Collins

1½ ounces gin
Lemon mix to fill glass; then shake
GLASS: Collins glass with ice
FRUIT: orange and cherry

Singapore Sling

1 ounce gin
¾ ounce sloe gin
¾ ounce cherry brandy
Lemon mix to fill glass; then shake
GLASS: Collins glass with ice
FRUIT: cherry

Recipes for Singapore Slings can vary greatly from bar to bar, and even among bartenders in the same bar. The gin and the lemon mix are always there, and it is always a tall drink, but the other ingredients have never become completely standardized.

Sloe Gin Fizz

1½ ounces sloe gin
Lemon mix to fill glass almost to the
    top; then shake

Club soda to fill up glass
GLASS: Collins glass with ice
FRUIT: cherry

Sombrero

1½ ounces coffee liqueur
Milk to fill glass; then shake
GLASS: highball, with ice

Sombreros are also sometimes served in a rocks glass, and with cream instead of milk. Sometimes the cream or milk is floated rather than shaken.

White Russian

1 ounce coffee liqueur
1 ounce vodka
Milk to fill glass; then shake
GLASS: Collins glass with ice

Like the Sombrero, the White Russian can also be served in a rocks glass, with just a splash of milk or cream.

COROLLARY DRINKS

John Collins. A tall Whiskey Sour, made in a Collins glass.

Ward 8. A tall Whiskey Sour, made in a Collins glass, with a splash of grenadine.

Vodka Collins. Use vodka instead of gin.

Bacardi Cocktail. A daiquiri made with Bacardi rum, and with a splash of grenadine syrup.

Virgin Mary. A Bloody Mary without vodka.

HOMEWORK: Make five each of the eleven basic shake drinks. For those drinks that can be made either up or on the rocks, make them both ways. Repeat, working for speed this time. Memorize the recipes, and the corollary drinks.

A Note on Lemon Mix

In older bartending guides you will sometimes see recipes calling for lemon juice and simple syrup. Simple syrup is sugar dissolved in water. It is very messy stuff and is no longer stocked by most bars. The trend today is to use a lemon mix—sometimes also called sour mix—that is pre-sweetened. Sour mix usually also contains a little egg white, or something to give it a good head.

You will find many bars in which the lemon mix does double duty, and is also used in drinks that, strictly speaking, should be made with lime juice. In these places, the only difference between a daiquiri and a rum sour is that the former gets a piece of lime, and the latter an orange and cherry.

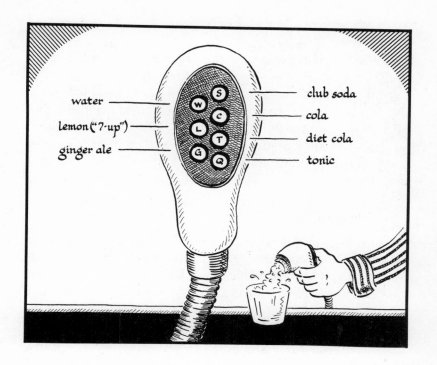

water — club soda

lemon ("7·up") — cola

ginger ale — diet cola

tonic

7. Build Drinks

BUILD DRINKS are made from ingredients that blend by themselves, without shaking or stirring. They are always made—or "built"—directly in the glasses in which they are served. In this category are all the standard highballs, like Rye and Ginger, Scotch and Soda, Gin and Tonic, Rum and Coke—the combinations are endless. Also in this category are the straight rocks drinks, like scotch on the rocks, or bourbon on the rocks. Stir drinks, like the Martini and the Manhattan, become build drinks when they are ordered on the rocks. Most bars pour a little less in their rocks drinks than in their up drinks. A Martini, for instance, might be 1½ ounces gin and ½ ounce vermouth on the rocks, instead of the 2 ounces gin and ½ ounce vermouth in the straight-up version.

Illustrated at the start of this chapter is a soda gun. One of the first things you should do when starting a new job is to find out what the letters on the buttons stand for, since the symbols often vary from one system to another. The gun above, with only seven buttons, is a small one. Some systems use several guns and have dozens of buttons, for sodas, juices, Bloody Mary mixes and lemon mixes, and wines.

The Highball

The highball was named after a railroad signal that came into use in the last part of the nineteenth century. A ball was placed on top of a pole to signal to the engineer that all was clear and he could proceed at full throttle. The signal was called a "highball" and railroad workers started using the term as a name for a Whiskey and Water, or a Whiskey and Soda. Today a highball can be any tall drink containing liquor and a mixer.

A highball is any drink made in a tall glass, with ice, and containing liquor and water or liquor and soda. Drinks like Gin and Tonic, Scotch and Soda, Whiskey and Ginger are all highballs. To make a highball, fill a highball glass with ice. The liquor is poured first, with one hand. The other hand operates the soda gun, and fills the glass the rest of the way with mixer. Add fruit, if any; then add stirrer and serve. Stirrers are always served with stir drinks.

A straight rocks drink—such as scotch on the rocks—is the simplest build drink of all. A shot of liquor is poured over ice in a rocks glass. Add fruit (if any is requested) and stirrer, and serve. The exact size of the shot depends on individual bar policy. Usually it is around 1½ ounces. In some establishments, the measure for rocks drinks is just visual, and the glass, after being packed with ice, is filled to, say, half an inch from the brim. If the glass is small, it is sometimes filled all the way to the brim.

The Old Fashioned is one build drink with a slightly more involved procedure.

Old Fashioned

1. Into an Old Fashioned glass (slightly larger than a rocks glass) put:
   - an orange slice and a cherry
   - teaspoon of sugar
   - few dashes of bitters
   - splash of club soda
2. Muddle—this means you stir the ingredients while squashing the fruit. Muddling is done with a pestle, or if this is not available, with the bar spoon.
3. Fill the glass with ice.
4. Add 1½ ounces whiskey.
5. Put a splash of club soda on top.

The fruit is sometimes added last, and not muddled. And the final splash of soda is sometimes omitted.

Screwdriver

1½ ounces vodka
Orange juice to fill glass
GLASS: highball, with ice

Tequila Sunrise

1½ ounces tequila
Splash of grenadine
Orange juice to fill glass
GLASS: Collins, with ice

Black Russian

1 ounce vodka

1 ounce coffee liqueur
GLASS: rocks glass, with ice

Rusty Nail

1½ ounces scotch
½ ounce Drambuie
GLASS: rocks, with ice

Mai Tai

1½ ounces rum
½ ounce crème de almond
Pineapple juice to fill glass
GLASS: Old Fashioned, with ice
FRUIT: pineapple slice and cherry

Planter's Punch

1 ounce rum
½ ounce apricot brandy
½ ounce triple sec
Splash of grenadine
Half and half grapefruit and orange
    juice, to fill glass
GLASS: Collins, with ice
FRUIT: orange slice

Like the Singapore Sling, the recipes for the Mai Tai and for Planter's Punch have many variants.

Irish Coffee

1½ ounces Irish whiskey
Hot coffee to fill glass
GLASS: coffee mug, or specialty glass
GARNISH: whipped cream

COROLLARY DRINKS

Harvey Wallbanger. A Screwdriver with ½ ounce Galliano floated on top.

Madras. A Screwdriver made with half orange and half cranberry juice.

Cape Cod. A Screwdriver made with cranberry instead of orange juice.

HOMEWORK: Make five each of the eight basic build drinks. Repeat, working for speed. Memorize the recipes, and the corollary drinks.

8. Blender Drinks

I PERSONALLY have never liked making drinks with the blender. Using the blender is time consuming, and it makes a horrible grating noise that destroys the tranquility of the barroom and interferes with television reception. Blender drinks are popular, however, especially with young people, and they are profitable. I will also admit that, when it is used with taste and imagination, the blender can produce some truly beautiful and delicious concoctions, some of which actually have nutritive value. Ice cream, fresh fruits, even vegetables can all be blended, either with or without liquor. It can be fun to experiment and come up with drinks to promote as house specialties.

Almost any standard drink can also be put in the blender, or "frozen." For example, a Margarita that has been blended is known as a Frozen Margarita, and so on.

You have to add a little more ice when you blend a drink, since you lose a little volume in the process. Frozen cream drinks, such as a Frozen Sombrero or a Frozen Brandy Alexander, can be given an extra richness if they are made with ice cream instead of regular cream or milk.

The Blue Moon

Randy Mullins, a seaman on the U.S.S. Fulton, had a dream one night aboard ship that he was at a bar with his favorite entertainers—Joan Baez, Linda Ronstadt, and Jethro Tull—and they were all drinking large blue cocktails. The next night Randy told his dream to Ronda Burke, a bartender at Anthony's Steam Carriage in New London, Connecticut. They tried together to capture the drink in the dream, at first unsuccessfully. Finally, Ronda made a Pina Colada, substituting blue curaçao for half of the rum. That was it! Randy's nickname on the Fulton was "Moon" Mullins, so they called the drink a Blue Moon.

Blend:
1 ounce rum
1 ounce blue curaçao
1 tablespoon coconut syrup
Pineapple juice
GLASS: *brandy snifter or specialty glass*
FRUIT: *orange slice*

The two blender drinks that have come to be standard calls are the Pina Colada and the Frozen Strawberry Daiquiri. It is hard to give exact amounts for these recipes, because the size of the glass varies from one bar to another. Some places will make them in brandy snifters, others in hurricane glasses or Collins glasses. You may have to discover the correct amounts of ice and juice by trial and error.

All the ingredients are placed directly in the blender cup, which is then put on the blender base. The cap is put on, the blender is turned on, and, after thirty seconds or so, the drink is ready.

Pina Colada

2 ounces rum
1 tablespoon coconut syrup
Pineapple juice
Ice
GLASS: brandy snifter or specialty
   glass
GARNISH: pineapple stick or cherry

Some places use a Pina Colada pre-mix, in which case you only add rum and ice.

Frozen Strawberry Daiquiri

2 ounces strawberry liqueur
¼ cup strawberries
Lime juice
Ice
GLASS: snifter or specialty glass
FRUIT: lime

Strictly speaking, a Daiquiri should be made with rum, but I find customer response is generally better when I use strawberry liqueur. Like the Pina Colada, Frozen Strawberry Daiquiris can also be made with a pre-mix.

COROLLARY DRINKS

Frozen Banana Daiquiri. Same as Frozen Strawberry Daiquiri, but made with half a banana and banana liqueur.

HOMEWORK: Memorize the recipes in this chapter. If you have a blender, buy some fresh fruit in season, some ice cream, and some rum. Experiment.

9. Review:
The Thirty Basic Cocktails

Stir Drinks

Martini
(Gibson)
Manhattan
(Rob Roy)
Gimlet
Stinger

Build Drinks

Screwdriver
(Madras)
(Harvey Wallbanger)
Black Russian
Tequila Sunrise
Old Fashioned
Rusty Nail
Mai Tai
Planter's Punch
Irish Coffee

Shake Drinks

Whiskey Sour
Daiquiri
(Bacardi Cocktail)
Margarita
Tom Collins
Bloody Mary
Sombrero
White Russian
Brandy Alexander
Grasshopper
Sloe Gin Fizz
Singapore Sling

Blender Drinks

Pina Colada
Frozen Strawberry Daiquiri

The thirty basic cocktails listed above, which have been covered in the past four chapters, are all the recipes that one really needs to start working as a professional bartender. On a busy night you might make as many as five hundred drinks. All but perhaps three of them would very likely be on this list—or else would be one of the standard highballs (Gin and Tonic, and so forth) or rocks drinks (scotch on the rocks, and so forth), or beer or wine or soda. Of the three remaining drinks, one might be something that *no one* has ever heard of (ordered by a customer who is playing stump-the-bartender); one might be a new drink that is just starting to be popular, or a drink that is just known locally; and the other one you will be able to look up quickly in the reference section at the end of this book.

Never be afraid to admit that you don't know how to make a drink. New drinks are "invented" every day, all over the country, and no one could possibly keep up with them all. Some drinks are created by the promotional staffs of liquor companies, in an attempt to sell more of their brand, and the recipe will be included in their advertisements. Some drinks are created by individual bars as house drinks. Some drinks are created by bartenders and/or their customers on slow nights. Once in a great while one of these drinks will become popular, sometimes only in one particular part of the country and sometimes nationally. Most new drinks, however, are forgotten as quickly as last night's wisecracks.

When someone asks me if I know how to make some drink I have never heard of, I say, "No, but I'll be glad to if you'll tell me what's in it." That's how bartenders learn new drinks. In fact, that's how some bartenders have learned all their drinks. When I hear a new drink recipe for the first time I make no conscious effort to memorize it, because I know from experience that nine times out of ten it will be a flash in the pan and never heard of again. If I get a second call for that drink, though, I always try to commit it to memory.

For a start, though, memorize the thirty basic cocktails. The drinks in the list that are in parentheses are *corollary drinks* of the drinks right above them. That is, there is only one ingredient that is different, but it causes the drink to have a different name. Not all of the corollary drinks listed in the past four chapters are included in the list of the thirty basic cocktails. Some of these other corollary drinks will no doubt sink in too, but don't worry too much about these for now.

Remember that while the amounts given are fairly standard, they may be slightly different at the bar where you work, because of either glass size or bar policy. My recipe for a Black Russian, for example, calls for 1 ounce vodka and 1 ounce coffee liqueur, in a rocks glass. You may work in a bar, however, where a rocks glass, when packed with ice, only holds 1½ ounces. In that case, obviously, a Black Russian would have ¾ ounce vodka and ¾ ounce coffee liqueur. My recipe for a Screwdriver calls for 1½ ounces vodka. But you may work in a bar where only 1 ounce is poured in highball-sized drinks. Exact pouring policies should be explained to you when you are hired. Sometimes you have to ask other bartenders.

A few of the recipes on this list are for drinks that are not completely standardized. You will find a different recipe for Planter's Punch, for instance, in almost any bartending guide in which you look. Basically, it is a rum and fruit juice drink, with a splash or two of some fruit-flavored cordials; but aside from that it is pretty much a fielder's choice. The Singapore Sling and the Mai Tai are also variable to some extent. For all of these drinks I have tried to give recipes that have ingredients that will be stocked by most bars, and that don't seem to be needlessly complicated. When you get a job, though, you should try to find out if there is a house recipe for drinks like these, or at least if there is agreement on what glasses to use.

Occasionally you will have a customer who sends back a drink saying, *"That's* not a Planter's Punch!" as if the correct recipe were on file with the Bureau of Standards. As you know, the customer is always right, and all you can do is to offer to make another drink.

HOMEWORK: Have someone quiz you on the thirty basic cocktails. If you miss one, look it up in the preceding four chapters, or in the reference section at the end of the book. Take the quiz again until your score is perfect.

10. Multiple Orders

A S A BARTENDER, you normally have direct contact with only a small part of your customers—those who sit at the bar. You will most likely also be making drinks for customers seated at tables, either in the lounge or the dining room. These orders will be given to you by waiters and waitresses, and on a busy night they can seem to come at you like the creatures in a Space Invaders game—the faster you make the drinks, the faster they seem to write out the orders. It is in this kind of situation—which can be fun if you know what you are doing—that you will need the information in this chapter.

Orders from waiters and waitresses will normally have more than one drink written on them, because people who are alone usually sit at the bar. Be prepared for all kinds of

---

Any man with a bottle in each hand can't be all bad.

—A CUSTOMER

---

abbreviations. An order for a Gin and Tonic, two Manhattans straight up, and a Whiskey Sour on the rocks, for example, might come to you like this:

$$G/T$$
$$②\ Man↑$$
$$W\ Sr\ Ⓡ$$

If they overdo this abbreviating, you just have to ask them what they mean.

Occasionally you will get an order that looks like this (Screw stands for Screwdriver and 7/7 for a Seven and Seven—Seagram's 7 and 7-Up):

$$Screw$$
$$7/7$$
$$Man↑$$
$$7/7$$
$$7/7$$
$$Screw$$

In this case you should tell the waiter or waitress that in the future, when a person in a party orders a drink that has already been ordered by someone else in that party, he or she should not write the drink over again, but should put a "2" in front of the first order. If someone else orders that drink again, the "2" should be made into a "3," and so on. The example above should have been written:

② Screw
③ 7/7
Man

This takes the waiter or waitress no longer, and can save you a lot of time.

Let's take Sample Order 1, which is for a Screwdriver and two Black Russians. The first thing you do when you get a multiple order is to *ice your glasses*. This gives you a few seconds to plan strategy. The Screwdriver is made in a highball glass, and for the Black Russians you will need to put ice into two rocks glasses.

Next, place the glasses with ice in them on your work surface in such a way that the glasses that will take common ingredients are "kissing"—that is, their rims are touching. In this order, all three drinks contain vodka, so they are all kissing. The two Black Russians also have coffee liqueur as a common ingredient, and they also kiss each other.

The reason for kissing your glasses is that it allows you to "run" your bottles. This means that you don't stop pouring between drinks, but just move the bottle quickly from one glass to the next, crossing over at the point where the rims touch.

When glasses of unequal height are kissed, you must start pouring with the taller glass, to avoid spillage. So we start pouring the vodka for the Screwdriver: One, two, three, four, five, *hup!* At *"hup!"* we run the vodka to the rocks glass, and simultaneously with the other hand we start pouring the coffee liqueur: One, two, three, *hup!* At this second *"hup!"* we run both bottles to the other rocks glass: One, two, three, *hup!* This time at *"hup!"* we "cut" or stop pouring both bottles. Now go back and pour the orange juice to finish the Screwdriver, and the order is complete.

Sample Order 2 is for a Vodka Gimlet on the rocks and two Gin Gimlets on the rocks. The liquors should be poured before the lime juice because the lime juice, being slightly heavier, would just sit on the bottom of the glass if it were poured first. Pour the vodka and the gin simultaneously into different glasses: One, two, three, four, five, *hup!* Then cut the vodka and run the gin to the next glass: One, two, three, four, five, *hup!* Last, run the sweetened lime juice across all three glasses: One, two, *hup,*one, two, *hup,* one, two, *hup!* Be sure to remember which one is the Vodka Gimlet, and tell the waiter or waitress.

Sample Order 3 is for two Scotch and Sodas and two Seven and Sevens. The two scotch glasses should be kissing, as should the two glasses for the Seven and Sevens. The scotch is poured with one hand, and the Seagram's 7 with the other: One, two three, four, five, *hup!* Then the bottles are simultaneously run to the next glass. Last, you add soda and 7-Up from the soda gun. You can run the soda just as if it were liquor. Again, remember which drinks are which, since Scotch and Sodas and Seven and Sevens look about the same. Sometimes it is a good idea to use different colors of stirrer to help you remember, particularly if the waiter or waitress has left to make a trip to the kitchen or some other place, and you will have made several other orders by the time this order is picked up.

Sample Order 4 is for two Whiskey Sours straight up. First, put a scoop of ice into a large mixing glass. Then pour three ounces of whiskey: One, two, three, four, five, six, seven, eight, nine, ten, *hup!* Next add lemon mix. If the lemon mix doesn't have a standard liquor pourer on it, you may have to estimate by eye. Then put the mixing cap on the shaker glass, shake, and strain into sour glasses. Fill the first glass most of the way, then the second glass most of the way, then even up with what is left.

Sample Order 5 is for two Whiskey Sours on the rocks. In this case the drinks are made directly in their serving glasses. First the whiskey is poured, running from one glass to the next. Next the lemon mix is poured, and this is also run. The drinks are then shaken separately. Add fruit and stirrers, unless this job is left to the waiters and waitresses in your establishment.

Sample Order 1.

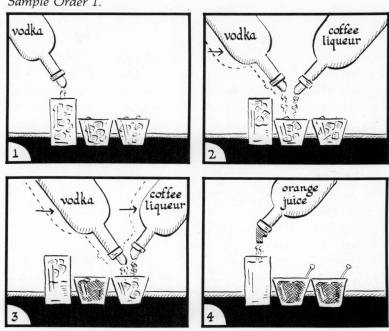

Order: Screwdriver, ② Black Russians

Sample Order 2.

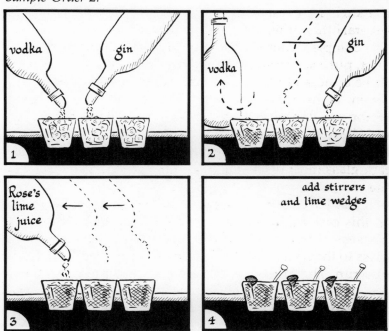

Order: Vodka Gimlet <u>Rocks</u>, ② Gin Gimlets <u>Rocks</u>

Sample Order 3.

Order : ② Seven and Seven, ② Scotch and Soda

Sample Order 4.

Order : ② Whiskey Sours <u>Straight Up</u>

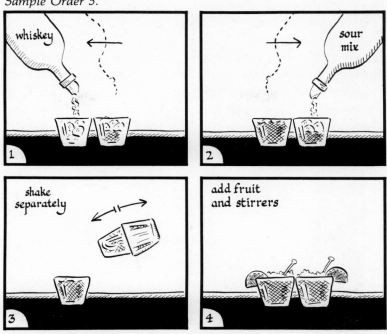

Order: ② Whiskey Sours <u>Rocks</u>

Most of the multiple orders you will get should fit into one of these patterns, or a combination of them. The basic principles are simple: that glasses with common ingredients are "kissed"; that each bottle you need is handled only once; and then you make use of the fact that you have two hands.

If an order has any shake drinks or draft beer in it, these should always be shaken or poured last, so that the head is still there by the time the drink reaches the customer. Blender drinks should always be made first, so that while the drink is in the machine you can be working on the rest of the order.

HOMEWORK: Using your home practice bar, make each of the sample orders five times. Then have someone make up multiple orders and call them out to you, or make them up yourself. Finally, go out to a well run bar on a busy night. Keep your eyes open.

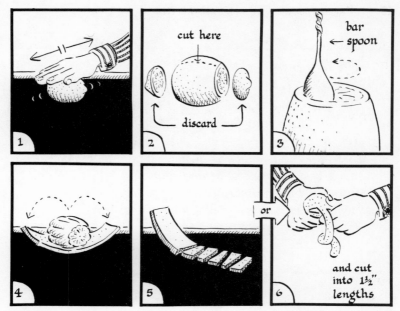

Lemon twists.

11. Fruit Slicing

IN THE BAR BUSINESS "fruit" can be used as a verb, as in, "The cocktail waitresses are sometimes required to fruit their own drinks."

Bartenders usually slice their fruit during slow periods. Sometimes the day shift, if that is the slow shift, will stock the supplies and prepare the fruit. The amount of fruit you cut depends on how busy you think it will be that shift, and this is something you will be able to estimate after you have been working at a place for a while. You should always cut enough fruit so that you are not caught short in the middle of a rush. On the other hand, you don't want to cut so much fruit that large amounts have to be thrown away. Some bars will discard all cut fruit at the end of the night. Others will put cut fruit in the cooler and use it the next day if it still looks presentable.

The Daiquiri

Around the turn of the century, Jennings Cox was an engineer at the Daiquiri Copper Mines near Santiago, Cuba. He was an amateur mixologist, and would entertain guests with a drink made from local produce: rum, limes, and sugar. The drink became known as a Daiquiri, and at first was primarily a local specialty of Havana. Ernest Hemingway was reportedly fond of Daiquiris, which may have given a boost to their popularity.

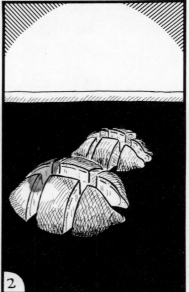

Lime wedges.

LIME WEDGES

A wedge of lime is served with any drink that contains tonic, such as Vodka and Tonic, Gin and Tonic, and Rum and Tonic; and in all Daiquiris.

The lime is first sliced in half along its axis, then in half again (see illustration). Each of these quarters is now sliced into anywhere from three to six pieces, depending on the size of the lime and the frugality of the management.

Limes may also be cut into slices, like oranges.

ORANGE SLICES

An orange slice and a cherry are served with all Sours, Collinses, and Old Fashioneds. A few drinks, such as a Screwdriver and a Planter's Punch, will take an orange slice alone.

First the ends of the orange are cut off. It is then sliced in half along its axis. Next, slit each half along its axis, as if you were going to cut the orange into quarters; but stop the cut short of the peel. (This slit will allow you to hang the slices on the rim of the glass.) Then slice each half into as many pieces as you wish.

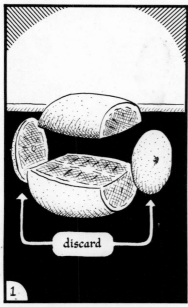
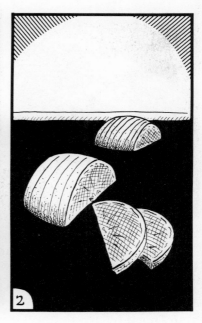

Orange slices.

CELERY STALKS

Celery stalks are used in most Bloody Marys.

Slice off the bottom of the bunch of celery so that it will fall apart into separate stalks. These must then be washed, and any wilted leaves at the top must be trimmed off. Some bars will then cut these stalks in half.

Celery stalks.

LEMON TWISTS

A "twist" is a small piece of lemon peel. It is served in Dry Manhattans and Perfect Manhattans, and it is often requested in Martinis in place of an olive. It is also sometimes requested in a rocks drink, as in "scotch on the rocks with a twist."

To cut twists, first roll the lemon back and forth under your hand while pressing down. This loosens the skin from the pulp. Then slice off the ends and discard them. Next, stick the bar spoon between the skin and the pulp on one end and cut all the way around (see illustration). Do the same on the other end. Now cut the skin as shown, and pull it away from the pulp. If the lemon is ripe, the skin should come away easily. Then cut the peel into short strips, which are the twists.

An alternate method is just to remove the peel with a knife or a peeler, and then cut it into 1½-inch lengths.

When serving a drink with a twist, rub the inside of the twist around the rim of the glass, and twist it over the drink. The essential oils are released as you twist—in the right light, you can actually see this as a burst of very fine spray. Then put the twist itself into the drink.

CHERRIES

Maraschino cherries are served in Manhattans and Rob Roys; along with oranges, they are also served in Sours, Collinses, and Old Fashioneds. They come in gallon jars, and are put into the fruit tray as needed, along with a little of their juice to keep them from drying out. The juice has a good flavor and can be used as a sweetener. If someone asks for a Manhattan on the sweet side I will sometimes put a little cherry juice in the Manhattan, along with extra sweet vermouth.

OLIVES

Unless the customer requests otherwise, Martinis are always served with a green olive. Usually the olive is served on a plastic "sword" or toothpick. Olives come packed in brine in large jars, and, like cherries, they are put into the fruit tray as needed. After they are taken out of the jar, olives should be lightly rinsed and kept in just a little water to keep them from drying out. If they are kept in the brine and not rinsed, some brine will be transferred to the Martini, and you will get an unappetizing brine slick floating on the surface of the drink.

12. Ice

BARS GENERALLY USE very small ice cubes, because that way it takes less liquor to fill the glass. For the same reason, the policy in most bars is to "pack" the glasses—that is, fill them as completely as possible. "Ice is cheaper than booze!" bar managers say.

Ice should always be fresh. Ice that has been out of the ice machine for too long will melt very quickly and dilute the drinks too quickly.

Bars that use small rocks glasses and fill them to the brim, or almost to the brim, will sometimes instruct their bartenders to overpack the ice in drinks going to the dining room or lounge, and fill them only three-fourths full with liquor. By the time the waitress or waiter has picked up the drink and put in a stirrer and fruit, and bounced it on a tray to the customer's table, the melting ice will have filled the drink the rest of the way (see illustration).

The Mai Tai

The first Mai Tai was created by Vic Bergeron—"Trader Vic"—at the service bar of his Oakland restaurant in 1944. It was first served to a friend of his from Tahiti, who took one sip and said, "Mai Tai—Roa Ae," which supposedly means in Tahitian, "Out of this world—the best!" The original recipe calls for:

> *1 ounce dark Jamaica rum*
> *1 ounce Martinique rum*
> *¼ ounce orgeat syrup*
> *½ ounce orange curaçao*
> *¼ ounce rock candy syrup*
> *1 lime*

The lime is first squeezed over shaved ice in a double Old Fashioned glass. The rest of the ingredients are then added, the drink is shaken, and it is decorated with the spent lime shell, fresh mint, and a pineapple stick.

You can still get a Mai Tai made according to the original recipe at any of the bars in the Trader Vic's chain. Most other places will serve a somewhat simplified, but not necessarily less potent, version. Because of the name, the Mai Tai went over big in Hawaii, where it has been known to be served with a small orchid for a garnish.

A scoop should always be used to put the ice into the glasses. Sometimes you will see bartenders scoop the ice with the glasses themselves. This saves time, but it should not be done; there is always the possibility that one of the glasses might be slightly chipped, and a piece of glass could be left in the ice. This is especially dangerous in a bar, because a customer who has had two or three drinks is very likely not to notice something like this, and to start chewing or even swallowing his ice cubes. For the same reason, whenever you break a glass you should always ask yourself if there is any possibility that a piece of glass may have landed in the ice. If there is, you must throw it out and get fresh.

Occasionally you may get a call for a "mist" or a "frappe," as in a Scotch Mist or a Crème de Menthe Frappe. This means a shot of that liquor poured over crushed ice—sort of an alcoholic snowcone. If your bar doesn't have an ice crusher, you can make do by putting a scoop of ice in the blender.

13. Beer

AFTER THE LOCATION of the rest rooms, the question you will be asked most frequently is, "What kinds of beer do you have?" You should memorize the beer list as soon as you start on a new job.

Normally a bar will carry both bottled beer and draft beer. Bottled beer is kept in a cooler, at a temperature between 36° and 45° F. Like wine glasses, glasses served with beer must be especially clean, since the glass is empty when the customer first sees it and any spots or streaks are very noticeable. Greasy glasses will also cause the head of the beer to collapse, as if it were flat. In more formal places, the first glass of beer is always poured into the glass for the customer. As a point of bar etiquette, a customer's beer bottle should not be removed until he or she has either ordered another one or left the bar, even though the bottle may be empty.

"Did you ever taste beer?"
"I had a sip of it once," said the small servant.
"Here's a state of things!" cried Mr. Swiveller. "She
never tasted it—*it can't be tasted in a sip!"*
—CHARLES DICKENS
The Old Curiosity Shop

At closing time it is usually the night bartender's job to restock the beer that has been used during that day. It sometimes happens that only the bottles on the top of the cooler will get replaced, and those on the bottom will stay there for months. Unlike some wines, however, bottled beer does not improve with age, and it can spoil if the stock in the cooler is not rotated occasionally.

Draft beer is preferred to bottled beer by many people, and for a bar the profits on draft beer are higher, but it is a little trickier to handle. If the temperature (36° to 38° F) or the pressure (12 to 14 pounds per square inch) are not correctly maintained, the beer will pour either flat or wild. When you pull the handle on the dispensing faucet, you must open it all the way. Beginning bartenders sometimes open the faucet only part way, out of caution, but this will cause the beer to pour too foamy. You also get too much foam if you hold the glass too far below the faucet, and allow the beer to pour straight into the bottom of the glass. Beer should be drawn so that the stream falls straight down the middle of the glass to *start* the head, and then the glass should be tilted, building the head from underneath. From day to day there will be slight variations in the way the draft is pouring, and you can compensate for this to some extent by how long you hold the glass straight up before you tilt it, and how far under the faucet you hold it. If the head on the beer is much more than one inch, you should pour a little off and top up the glass with more beer.

TYPES OF BEER

Barley malt, yeast, hops, and water are the traditional ingredients of beer. Sometimes other grains are also used, such as corn, rice, or wheat. These ingredients can be combined in different proportions, and put through different brewing processes to produce several types of beer.

Lager beer. This is the standard American beer, served at beaches and baseball games. It is pale colored and light in flavor. Most of the European imports are also lagers, but the flavor is usually a little stronger than the American mass-market beers.

Pilsner beer. In theory, this means beer that is similar to that brewed in Pilsen, Czechoslovakia, but in fact it is more often just another name for lager.

Dark beers. These are usually also lagers, but generally they are sweeter, heavier, and more malty.

Ale. Ale is brewed at a higher temperature than lager, so that the yeast floats at the top of the vat, rather than settling. The hops flavor is stronger in ale than in lager.

Stout. Stout is a kind of ale that is extremely dark, malty, and rich, with a strong flavor of hops and sometimes slightly sweet. Ireland's Guinness is probably the most famous of the stouts.

Porter. A dark beer that is somewhere between ale and stout in flavor.

Weisser beer. Also called weizenbier or weiss beer. This is a wheat-based beer that, in Germany, is sometimes served with a shot of raspberry syrup in the bottom of the glass.

Malt liquor. In the United States, beers with more than five percent alcohol must use this name.

Light beer. This is beer with fewer calories than regular lager. It also has slightly less alcohol, and, unfortunately, less flavor.

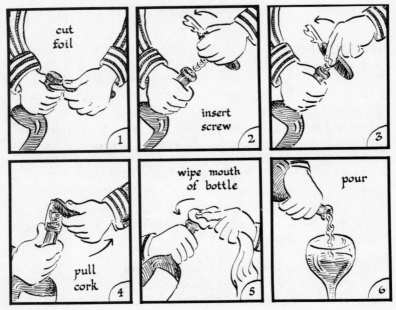

Opening wine.

14. Wine

FOR WINES that can be ordered by the glass most bars offer, at a minimum, a white wine, a red wine, and a rosé. These are usually inexpensive wines, poured from a gallon jug. In a place that sells a lot of wine, it may come from a keg and be dispensed by a gun that is similar to the soda gun. In bars attached to good restaurants, and in bars where the patrons are likely to be more discriminating about wine, several types of red and several types of white may be offered by the glass. The whites and the rosés are always served chilled—that is, they are kept in the cooler. The reds are served at room temperature.

The normal serving of wine in bars is between five and six ounces. If a standard eight-ounce wine glass is used, this means it will be filled about three-quarters full. If a ten-ounce tulip glass is used, it will only be filled about half full. Wines served by the glass can usually also be ordered by the carafe. These generally come in liter and half-liter sizes.

Drink no longer water, but use a little wine for thy stomach's sake.

—St. Paul
Epistle to Timothy, V, 23

SERVING A BOTTLE OF WINE

In bars with wine lists, the bartender may have to serve wine that is ordered by the bottle. The procedure is as follows:

1. The bottle is shown to the customer so that he can see the label. This is to verify that the bottle you are about to serve is the one he ordered.
2. Cut away the foil around the lip of the bottle, using the knife on your corkscrew.
3. Try to keep the corkscrew in line with the center of the cork as you screw it in.
4. Place the metal foot of the corkscrew against the lip of the bottle and hold it there with the thumb of the hand holding the bottle (see illustration). This gives you a point of leverage, and the other hand tilts the handle of the corkscrew, which withdraws the cork. After the cork is out of the bottle by an inch or so, pull it the rest of the way with your hand.
5. Wipe the mouth of the bottle with a cloth or napkin.
6. Pour a little into the glass of the person who ordered the wine. This person tastes the wine first—to make sure it is not spoiled—and then the rest of party is served, and the taster's glass filled to its proper level.

Unlike wine ordered by the glass, wine ordered by the bottle is poured so that the glass is only about half full.

When serving your least expensive bottle of artificially carbonated wine with a screw cap, the above ritual may be somewhat abbreviated.

Opening champagne.

OPENING CHAMPAGNE AND SPARKLING WINE

When wine is under pressure it requires a different opening technique:

1. Loosen the wire hood, and remove the hood, along with the top of the foil capsule.
2. Holding the cork firmly in the palm of one hand, twist the bottle with the other hand. This usually loosens the cork enough so that it pops out by itself, and your hand keeps it from landing in an inappropriate place. If the cork doesn't come out by itself, pull a little as you twist.

3. Fill glasses about two-thirds full. Keep the bottle on ice between servings, either in an ice bucket, or, if the customer is sitting right at the bar, in your ice bin.

DESSERT WINES

The "house" wines—those sold by the glass and the carafe—and the wines on the wine list are all *table wines,* which means they are naturally fermented from grape juice, with no other significant flavorings or additions, and contain 14 percent alcohol or less. There are also the so-called *dessert wines.* These are sweet wines whose alcoholic content has been raised by the addition of brandy or other spirits. They are usually kept on the back bar along with the other liquor bottles, and it may be useful to know something about them. They all may be ordered either straight up or on the rocks. When ordered straight up they are usually served in a three-ounce sherry glass.

Port. Port is a wine whose fermentation has been stopped before it is finished by the addition of high-proof grape brandy. It is rich, sweet, and wonderfully warming in cold weather. Ruby port is deep red, and tawny port is amber colored.

Sherry. Sherry is also fortified by the addition of brandy. It is fermented and aged in 158-gallon casks of white oak, where it forms on its surface a crust of yeast known as *flor,* which is partly responsible for its unique flavor.

Vermouth. Both dry vermouth, which is pale in color, and sweet vermouth, which is darker, are sometimes taken straight, as well as in Martinis and Manhattans. They are most often ordered on the rocks, with a twist. These are also fortified wines, and they are both flavored with herbs and aromatics, including Artemisia flowers, orange peel, chamomile, and anise.

Dubonnet. Sweet, red *aperitif* wine flavored with herbs and quinine.

DRINKS MADE WITH WINE

There are also mixed drinks made with wine, the most common of these being the Spritzer, the Wine Cooler, and the Kir.

Spritzer (build)

2/3 parts white wine
1/3 part club soda
GLASS: Collins, with ice

Wine Cooler (build)

Red wine
Splash of lemon mix
GLASS: Collins with ice

Kir (build)

5 ounces white wine
1/2 ounce crème de cassis
GLASS: wine glass

pot still used in
making scotch whiskey

condenser →
← distillate

"distiller's
beer"

heat source

15. Liquor

DRINKS CAN BE ORDERED either by generic name or brand
name. For instance, a customer may order "Scotch and
Soda" or "Dewar's and Soda." For the "Scotch and Soda"
you will use *bar scotch*. This is generally an inexpensive,
relatively unknown brand. It is usually kept in the speed
well, which is right in front of the bartender, along with the
other bar liquors. For "Dewar's and Soda" you will pour the
drink, obviously, with Dewar's White Label, which is a
popular brand of scotch. This is a *call brand*, which means
one that is only poured when the customer orders that
particular brand, and for which he or she is charged extra.
The other major category is *top shelf* liquor. This is often
kept literally on the top shelf of the back bar, to remind the
bartender that this is the most expensive category. Things
like twelve-year-old scotch and cognac are always top
shelf, along with certain of the cordials.

For each of the major liquors, then, you will have a *bar brand*, one or more *call brands*, and possibly a *top shelf* brand. This will be true for vodka, gin, rum, whiskey, bourbon, and scotch, at the least. You also may have bar and call brands of tequila, brandy, coffee liqueur, and amaretto. For the less frequently ordered liquors—ouzo, for example— you will generally have only one brand, and usually it will be priced as a call brand, even though the brand name may not be requested by the customer.

The "proof" of liquor is a simple code that tells the alcoholic content. The percentage of alcohol is equal to half the proof. So a 100 proof liquor (also written 100°) contains 50 percent absolute alcohol. Most liquors are around 86 proof. Some of the cordials go as low as 40 proof, and some of the rums as high as 151 proof. These last should not be poured near an open flame.

Claret is the liquor for boys, port for men; but he who aspires to be a hero must drink brandy.

—DR. SAMUEL JOHNSON

TYPES OF LIQUOR

Liquors start out as low-proof fermented liquids, similar to a kind of flat beer. This liquid is then distilled—that is, part of it is boiled off and collected again, and the alcohol is concentrated in this part. During this process, and the aging that follows, the liquor will acquire certain flavors, and others may be added intentionally. It is not necessary for a bartender to know a great deal about how liquors are made, but a short description of the basic types might be helpful in keeping them distinct in your mind.

Vodka. Vodka is a clear liquor that is nothing more than ethyl alcohol diluted with water. It is made from grain, and is distilled and redistilled until there is nothing left of the flavor of the original ingredients. Because it has very little taste of its own, it goes well with juices and mixers. Another reason for its popularity is that it leaves no smell on the breath. Some popular call brands are Smirnoff, Gordon's, Stolichnaya, and Absolut.

Gin. Gin is another clear liquor. It is basically a kind of flavored vodka. The exact combination of herbs, seeds, and peels used for flavoring varies from one brand to another, but the flavor of juniper berries always predominates. Many of the best-known gins are imported from England, which is the original home of gin. Well-known brands are Beefeater, Booth's, Gordon's, Tanqueray, and Boodles.

Rum. Rum is distilled from sugar cane, and is usually produced in tropical countries where sugar cane is a major crop, particularly in the countries of the Caribbean. There are both light rums, which are clear in color and light in flavor, and dark rums, which are heavier and sweeter. Popular call brands are Bacardi, Ronrico, Mount Gay, and Myer's.

Tequila. Tequila is made in Mexico from the agave plant, which looks something like an enormous pineapple. It can be either clear or amber colored. The latter is called "gold" and the color comes from aging in wood. Drinkers of straight tequila will sometimes ask for salt and lime, which is part of this peculiar drinking ritual:

1. Place salt on the web of the hand between thumb and forefinger, holding a piece of lime in the same hand. The other hand holds the shot of tequila.
2. Lick salt.
3. Do shot.
4. Bite lime.

Some call brands of tequila are Jose Cuervo, Sauza, and Herradura.

Brandy. Brandy is a liquor that is distilled from wine. When ordered straight up it is served in a brandy snifter, a glass that concentrates the strong, complex bouquet. Cognac is a type of brandy that comes from the Cognac region of southwestern France. Some American brandies are Christian Brothers, Paul Masson, and Coronet. Some call brands of cognac are Hennessy, Courvoisier, Martell, and Remy Martin.

Whiskey. Whiskey, like vodka, is distilled from a mash of grain and water, but here the distillation is done in such a way that some of the flavor of the original mash is retained. There are many different kinds of whiskey—scotch, bourbon, Canadian, and so forth—and a complete understanding of all the differences in their various distillation processes would almost require a graduate degree in chemistry. Below I will just give a few of the principal characteristics of each type.

Blended whiskey. Blended whiskey is a blend of straight whiskey and grain neutral spirits—which is another name for vodka. It has, therefore, a lighter taste than straight whiskey, and it is usually less expensive. Blended whiskey is almost never ordered by its proper name. Some customers will just ask for whiskey, and it is understood that they want a blended whiskey, rather than a bourbon or a scotch or one of the other whiskies. Blended whiskey is also sometimes called "rye." There actually are straight rye whiskies, but they are not very common, and they will normally be requested as call brands. When you get an order for "Rye and Ginger" or "Whiskey and Water" you can be certain that a blended whiskey is what is expected. Some call brands are Seagram's 7, Fleischmann's, Calvert, Schenley, and Kessler.

Bourbon whiskey. Kentucky is the birthplace of bourbon, and 80 percent still comes from that state. By law, the grains used in making bourbon must be at least 51 percent corn. For some reason, makers of bourbon often call their product "old" something-or-other. Some call brands are Old Grand-dad, Old Taylor, Old Forester, Old Fitzgerald, Old Crow, Early Times, and Jim Beam.

Tennessee whiskey. Tennessee whiskey is similar to bourbon. One distinction is that Tennessee whiskey is always filtered through maple charcoal. There are only two brands: Jack Daniel's and George Dickel.

Rye whiskey. Rye whiskey is distilled primarily from rye grain. I know of one brand: Old Overholt.

Scotch whisky. The Scots named whiskey—it means "the water of life" in Gaelic—and they have been making it since the middle ages. They spell it without the "e"—whisky. Most scotches are a blend of malt whiskey and grain whiskey. The grain whiskey is similar to American and Canadian grain whiskey. The malt whiskey is made from barley malt—sprouted barley grain—that is dried slowly on screens over smoldering peat fires. The malt takes on a flavor from this peat smoke, which is one of the things responsible for the unique taste of scotch. Some of the more expensive scotches are made entirely from malt whiskey. There are hundreds of brands of scotch. Some of the better known ones are Dewar's, Cutty Sark, J & B, Black and White, Bell's, Johnny Walker, Ballantine's, The Glenlivet, Glenfiddich, and Chivas Regal.

Irish whiskey. Like scotch, Irish whiskey contains some malt whiskey, but the Irish malt is not permitted to absorb the flavor of the peat smoke. It is triple distilled and very smooth. In 1966 the three main Irish distilleries merged, and almost all Irish whiskey is now produced by one company, Irish Distillers, Ltd. The principal export brands are Jameson's, Old Bushmill's, and Murphy's.

Canadian whisky. The differences between Canadian whisky (spelled without the "e," like scotch) and American blended whiskey are quite minor. Some well-known call brands are Canadian Club ("C.C."), Seagram's V.O., and Crown Royal.

brandy
snifter

cordial
pony

16. Cordials

CORDIALS, also called liqueurs, are sweet, flavored liquors. When ordered straight up they are either served
in a pony, which is a kind of elegant shot glass, or a brandy
snifter. The brandy snifter is designed so that when it is put
on its side it will hold exactly a shot (usually 1½ ounces).
You can use this fact to check your pouring. If you are asked
to warm the snifter, you can rinse it out with very hot water
and flick it dry. This increases the evaporation of the cordial
slightly, which enhances its "nose."

Below is a list of the cordials you are most likely to
encounter, and the principal flavor, or flavors, of each. It is
a gross oversimplification to describe the taste of some of
these elixirs in two or three words, but it should serve as an
initial orientation. If you are curious to know more, have a
sip.

The Kir

This was the favorite aperitif of Canon Felix Kir, a French clergyman, socialist, and Resistance fighter who was for a time the mayor of Dijon. It consists of a splash of crème de cassis in a glass of white wine.

Amaretto: almond
Anisette: anise (licorice)
Bailey's Irish Cream: Irish whiskey, heavy cream
Benedictine: cognac, herbs
B & B: Benedictine, brandy
Blackberry Brandy: blackberries, brandy
Blue Curaçao: orange peel
Campari: quinine
Chambord: raspberry
Chartreuse: herbs, brandy
Cherry Brandy: cherries, brandy
Cherry Heering: cherries
Coffee Liqueur: coffee
Cointreau: orange peel, brandy
Crème de Bananes: banana
Crème de Cacao: chocolate
Crème de Cassis: black currants (raisins)
Crème de Menthe: mint
Crème de Noyau: almond
Curaçao: orange peel
Drambuie: scotch, honey, herbs
Frangelico: hazelnuts
Galliano: vanilla, anise, citrus
Grand Marnier: brandy, orange peel
Irish Mist: Irish whiskey, honey, heather
Kahlua: coffee
Kirsch: cherries
Kummel: caraway seeds
Midori: honeydew melon
Ouzo: anise

Peppermint Schnapps: peppermint
Pernod: anise
Peter Heering: cherries
Rock and Rye: rye whiskey, rock candy
Sabra: chocolate, orange
Sambuca: anise, elderberry
Sloe Gin: sloeberries
Southern Comfort: whiskey, peaches
Strega: herbs, citrus
Tia Maria: coffee
Vandermint: chocolate, mint

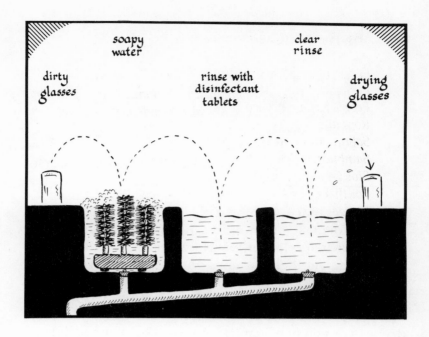

dirty glasses

soapy water

rinse with disinfectant tablets

clear rinse

drying glasses

17. Cleaning

AT LEAST HALF OF BARTENDING is cleaning of one sort or another, and I think you will find that your professional reputation depends as much on how well you clean as on anything else. You may mix drinks faster than anyone, and have the personality of Falstaff, but if the bar always looks slovenly while you are working and you leave a mess for the bartender who works after you, your name will be mud. Being clean is a good way to compensate for your flaws as a bartender.

A lot of cleaning can be done in your "down" time, that is, while you are waiting for your next order. Personally, I sort of enjoy cleaning, and would rather be busy with small, mechanical tasks than stand like a dummy waiting to make the next drink. Most bar cleaning is fairly light work that doesn't interrupt any conversations you may be having—unless you want it to.

A mirror not covered with dust is clear and bright. The mind should be like this. When what beclouds it passes away, its brightness appears.

—KOJISEI
Vegetable Root Discourses

Your primary cleaning tool is your "barmop"—a cloth that you keep slightly wet, but not so wet that it actually leaves water droplets on a surface after you wipe it. Some bartenders wet their barmops with club soda. This works fairly well as a cleaning agent, but I use plain warm water, and just a touch of soapy water from the sink. You may find that you prefer to use two barmops—one wet, and one for drying—or you may just use one, and keep one end damp and one end dry. You will use it to wipe down the bar after the departure of all but the neatest customers.

Ashtrays should be emptied periodically, and cleaned completely after the customer leaves. This can be done with the customer's used cocktail napkin. You should not use your barmop to clean ashtrays, because it will get dirty too quickly. If your bar uses coasters instead of cocktail napkins, you should keep a separate cloth or paper towel for ashtrays.

In matters like wiping the bar and cleaning ashtrays, you have to maintain a scale of priorities. If you are working a slow afternoon shift, for instance, accompanied only by three or four regular customers, you will have all the time you need to keep the ashtrays clean. But then if a party of fifty suddenly walks in, and there is no cocktail waitress, the priorities will change. The most important thing now is getting the drinks out, and getting the money in. When you get caught up you can think about cleaning ashtrays and wiping the bar. If in the midst of this rush you see some ashtrays that are particularly full, you might just dump them, without worrying about cleaning them thoroughly at that point.

Some bartenders are fortunate enough to work in places where the glasses are sent to the kitchen and put through the dishwashing machine. All you have to do in this case is to stack the glasses in the plastic dishwashing racks, and take them out when they come back from the kitchen. Most of us, however, still wash all our glasses in the bar.

In a three-sink system, the first sink holds the dishwashing machine, which consists of spinning brushes. This sink is filled with detergent and hot water. The second sink is a rinse containing disinfectant tablets, and the third is a clear rinse. In a two-sink system, the last sink would be eliminated, or used as a drain sink.

The glasses should be pushed down over the center brush. This allows the outer brushes to clean the outside of the glass. Before you put each glass into the water, check it for lipstick. Often the brushes alone will not remove lipstick, and you will have to rub the rim of the glass a little with your fingers in the soapy sink.

When your water gets cold and dirty, the sinks must be emptied and refilled with fresh detergent and water. On very busy nights, it may seem impossible to do this. Don't give in to the temptation to wash your glasses in dirty water, but try to keep your water clean and hot as long as possible. Run the water as hot as you can stand it when you fill the sink. And don't use too much soap. If you overdo the soap, you will very quickly have three soapy sinks and no rinse.

The things that will contaminate your water the quickest are cream drinks—like Sombreros and Brandy Alexanders—and syrup drinks—like Pina Coladas and Frozen Strawberry Daiquiris. It doesn't take much of these mixtures in your rinse water to cause your glasses to dry with streaks. When you have to rinse out your shaker cap after making a cream drink, you should not dip it in the rinse sink, as you might after making something like a Whiskey Sour. Instead, you should fill it from the tap, and then empty it in the drain. The same is true of the blender cup. And you should never wash ashtrays in the sink, unless it is the very last thing you do at night before draining the sinks.

If your glasses do get streaks and spots on them, you can get rid of this after they dry by polishing them. I find a clean paper towel or cocktail napkin works best for polishing, unless you want to look like the bartenders in the cartoons, who always seem to polish glasses with a cloth.

In addition to the things that have to be cleaned dozens and sometimes hundreds of times a night, there are also cleaning jobs that need to be done at longer intervals. If you use the kind of arrangement, for instance, where stemmed glasses are hung upside down over the bar, every few days you must take down and wash any glasses that haven't been used recently. Otherwise they will get clouded by tobacco smoke.

Sometimes wine carafes will get stained inside, where it is almost impossible to scrub them. These can be filled with water containing a teaspoon or so of ammonia, left overnight, and emptied and rinsed in the morning.

The pourers on the liquor bottles should be taken off and soaked in the sink once a week or so, particularly those on the sweet liquors. The ice should be removed from the ice bins at least once a week, and the bins cleaned out. (This is a job that must be done before opening or after closing.) Once every few weeks or so the beer and wine cooler should be emptied and cleaned. Baking soda is good for this. The fruit trays will often need cleaning, as will the speed well and the shelves on which the glasses and bottles are kept.

These occasional cleaning jobs are usually shared by all the bartenders, and the more of these things you can find time to do, the more you will be loved by management and your fellow bartenders. You should also be on the lookout for new places to clean—little neglected areas where, over time, things might accumulate that would attract insects and bacteria.

At the end of the night, the closing bartender will go through a final cleaning. Everything will be removed from the bar surface. The juices and fruits will be put away in the cooler, and the bar implements—shaker caps, strainer, and so forth—will be stacked on the back bar or next to the sink. Then the stripped bar surface is wiped down completely. The ashtrays should now be washed. A final "Soapa-Colada" should be made to clean the blender, and the blender should be rinsed. The sinks should be drained, and then scoured so that no ring is left. All stainless steel surfaces should be cleaned, and then dried so they are not spotted when they dry. Take out the garbage. Remember that the daylight of the following morning will reveal with stark clarity things that were barely visible when you left at night.

18. Customer Relations: The Fun Part

DURING YOUR FIRST few days working a new bar you usually feel a little self-conscious. This is normal. Gradually you begin to loosen up and feel comfortable with your bar and its patrons. Some you will see only once and yet always remember. Some will treat you like a piece of furniture, and some will treat you like an oracle. With some of the regulars you will develop a relationship that has all the complexity and nuance of friendship.

Remember that anyone can buy a bottle and drink more cheaply at home. Sometimes a simple hello can make the difference in whether they do just that or whether they stop in where you are working. Try to remember names. When someone introduces himself or a friend, reach your hand across the bar. Compliment people on their new car, their new hat, their pictures of their children. Laugh at their jokes.

But while you must appear friendly, you must also learn never to be intrusive. A bartender, for instance, can never go up to people and ask them what they do for a living, like someone at a cocktail party. Nor can you suddenly butt into a conversation on which you have been eavesdropping. One of the things that makes bartending fun is all that you overhear. But you must never indicate that you are listening.

It is very bad form, of course, to correct a customer, unless you know him or her very well. Alcohol has a tendency to make some people start their mouths before their brain is in gear, but that, to a certain extent, is what bars are for.

If customers are with friends it is generally best to let them entertain themselves, unless you know them, or unless they speak to you. If a customer is alone and it is not too busy you might offer some opener—a comment on the weather, or the Kentucky Derby, or whatever. There will be some customers, naturally, who do not feel like talking, and some days when you will feel the same way.

When I work I alternate my greetings according to what seems right at the time—"Hi, how are you?" or, "May I help you?" or, "What'll it be, George?"—as I slide forward the cocktail napkin.

Then they give you their order, and sometimes you have to ask a clarifying question, such as "Up or on the rocks?"

Next you make their drinks: get glasses, ice them, pour booze, add fruit and/or stirrer. Place drinks on cocktail napkins.

If the customer looks as though he is reaching for his wallet, tell him the price of the drink: "That will be $1.75, please." Otherwise, you will generally make out a tab. (See Chapter 20, Cash Register Technique.)

When you are offered money, announce the size of the bill, such as, "Out of five," or "Out of twenty." This prevents both you and the customer from forgetting the amount tendered.

When you count out change, keep the big bills on the bottom of the stack. Some customers like to leave their money on the bar, and it is more secure that way.

When you see an empty glass, ask if the customer wants another drink, but do not give him or her a feeling of being rushed. Never remove customers' glasses before they leave, unless they have been shut off and are beginning to be a problem.

Avoid topics of conversation that could lead to an argument. If one of your customers thinks we should go to war with Patagonia, let him express his opinion, but keep yours to yourself. Chances are that in the morning he will remember neither, and it is not worth risking an unpleasant situation.

When you get a phone call for a customer, put it on hold before asking if he or she is "there."

If customers offer to buy you a drink, tell them no thanks, you've got a long night ahead. Drinking while you work can be a bad habit for bartenders. You tend to give away free drinks and break glasses. If you do allow yourself a drink near to closing time, it looks better to have it in a soda glass.

The Margarita

The Margarita was invented by a Los Angeles bartender in 1954, in a drink competition sponsored by tequila manufacturers.

Unless you know the customers, it is best to offer them last call at least 25 minutes before you actually close. This avoids last-minute tug-of-wars with "cling-ons"—people who get childish about giving up their glass at the end of the night. As you gain experience, you will be able to spot potential cling-ons, and offer them last call a little early.

Sometimes, when you see that people are forgetting to finish their drinks and it is getting close to closing, you have to give them a countdown: "Ten minutes, folks!" Then, "Five minutes, folks!" And finally, "You don't have to go home, folks, but you can't stay here!"

19. Problem Customers

WHEREVER PEOPLE DRINK, even in the most elegant and expensive places, there are occasional problem customers. With experience you can learn to handle these people with a minimum of disturbance to yourself and your other customers. You will also learn to know the local "characters." Some of them may be basically all right in spite of their eccentricities, while others are chronic troublemakers and should never be served under any circumstances.

People get shut off for two basic reasons. The first is because, in your judgment, they have reached a point of intoxication where they might injure themselves or others. This is a matter of personal judgment, although it is often influenced, to some extent, by the standards of the individual bar—some are more tolerant of slightly intoxicated behavior than others. The bartender can also be a little more indulgent with a customer who he knows will not be driving. The second reason people get shut off is because, regardless of how much they have had to drink, they are becoming obnoxious to you or your customers.

The first type of shut-off is usually no problem—a quiet, "I'm sorry, sir [or ma'am], but I think you've had enough," and they generally leave respectably. Occasionally, when shut off, the first type turns into the second type.

Often you will get customers who have been shut off at another bar first. Usually the walk between the last bar and yours sobers them up a little, and when they walk in they summon up all their resources in an attempt to give an impression of sobriety. Sometimes they get away with it, and you serve them. As soon as they get their drink, naturally, they fall apart again. If they are not too disgraceful, I may let these types finish the drink I have made for them. Sometimes they realize that they will not get a second drink, and go away without even asking.

If you are unsure about the sobriety of a younger customer, you can ask for proof of age. This gives you a few extra seconds to judge how drunk the person is.

Once or twice I have mistakenly refused service to someone who was not drunk at all. Perhaps they were just tired, or they might have had a partial paralysis or some other condition that at first seemed to me like intoxication. These people have usually been either slightly amused or slightly embarrassed by the situation, but they never have that wounded outrage of the drunk who has just been told that he can no longer be served. In general, the more angrily someone protests being shut off, the more you were justified in doing it.

Try to get the point across in a way that avoids embarrassment. One thing that sometimes works is to total the customer's bill and present it to him, hoping that he will get the message that way.

Inevitably, though, there will be customers who simply must be told that you can no longer serve them. Never say something like, "Don't you think you've had enough?" This sounds like you want to discuss the matter with them, and discussions between bartenders and customers they have shut off are always awkward and pointless. If possible, tell them in such a way that other people cannot hear, and then walk away.

Once in a great while, the situation will go one step beyond this, and the customer you have shut off will refuse to leave and will sit there shouting personal remarks at you. One time I was literally cursed, by a woman who claimed to be a voodoo priestess, and who danced around the bar as she asked the spirits to destroy me. Other customers have responded to being shut off by questioning my sexual orientation, and so on. These customers should simply be asked to leave. If they refuse, and they happen to be very drunk and very small, you may sometimes want to throw them out yourself. Legally, you have a right to use "reasonable force" to remove a customer who is causing a disturbance and refuses to leave when asked, as long as it is not your intent to harm that person. This is known in the trade as the "bum's rush." Otherwise, you should call the manager or the bouncer, or, if they are not available, the police. You should have the police's number written down right next to the phone, or, better still, know it by heart.

I don't want to overemphasize this aspect of bartending. Weeks and months can go by without any serious disturbances, and when they do come, nine times out of ten the only thing that happens is the release of a little hot air. With experience you develop the ability to sense imminent trouble, and this can be helpful because it gives you time to prepare yourself.

When confronted by an abusive customer, your body may provide you with a quick shot of adrenalin that will cause your pulse rate to quicken, and you may feel anger, or fear, or some combination of these. This is a normal reaction to stress and can be helpful to you by increasing your alertness, but on the other hand you don't want to reach the point where you lose your composure.

Here is what I do when I am in a situation that makes me feel in danger of blowing my cork:

First, I use the old technique of counting slowly to ten (to myself), while taking deep breaths. This can prevent you from saying or doing something that is just as stupid, if not more so, as the behavior of the customer in question. With every count, I try to imagine my adrenalin barometer dropping.

Second, I practice "centering." This is an old Japanese martial-arts technique. What you do is visualize your center of gravity. This is a point about two inches below the navel and two inches inside the body. Stand straight, but relaxed, balancing your body around this point. As you count to ten, breathing deeply, let all your feelings of fear, anger, or panic drain out through this center point. This may sound totally ridiculous, which may be partly why it works.

Third, I think about my grapes. In my back yard I have some grapevines, and caring for them is my favorite hobby. Being outside on a nice day pruning or watering seems very far away from the other kinds of work I do, including bartending, and that is part of the reason I enjoy it. Thinking about my grapes while dealing with irate customers helps me to keep things in perspective.

In difficult situations, the more crowded the bar, the more secure you will feel, since the other customers will take the side of the bartender against anyone making a disturbance. Unless you are sure you know what you are doing, avoid exposing yourself to the risk of injury or lawsuit: stay behind the bar.

20. Tips

TO SOME EXTENT, the amount of your tip is related to how friendly you are to your customers, but I have always felt that giving undue attention to this fact is a little too much like selling yourself. I think it is a better policy to give good service to everyone, and not to count your tips until the end of the night. Until that point, sweep the money up as if it were stray peanuts. It is a waste of energy to gnash your teeth every time you are "stiffed"—that is, left no tip. And these customers are usually balanced out by customers who are arbitrarily generous.

The origin of tipping goes back to feudal times. A customer at an inn would pay the innkeeper for his food and drink, and then he would leave a few small coins for the servants. If he didn't, he might find foreign bodies in his gruel on his next visit. Today, waiters and waitresses

80

and bartenders are no longer in a different social class from their customers, and tips are just another form of income. In the minds of some people, though, there is still something slightly demeaning about working for tips. You can see this in the way they go about tipping.

The Singapore Sling

This drink was created at the Raffles Hotel in Singapore at the beginning of this century. Recipes for the Singapore Sling vary, but it is always a tall drink with gin, cherry brandy, and lemon juice. Some bartenders will add to these basic ingredients some sloe gin, or bitters, or a few drops of Benedictine.

Some people, for instance, will leave the tip hidden under the cocktail napkin—"the tooth fairy syndrome." Some, after getting their change at the register, will go back and leave their tip where they were sitting. It would be easier to give you the tip at the register, but presumably they find the transaction slightly embarrassing. For the same reason, some customers will avoid speaking directly about your tip. So instead of saying something like "Keep the change," they will say something ambiguous like "That's fine." Unless you are completely sure what this means, you should give back the change. Otherwise, you will have to fish it out of your tip jar, and that *is* embarrassing.

One time I had to shut a man off, and he was furious with me. Having paid his bill, which was quite large, he picked up his quarter in change. He looked at the quarter, he looked at me, he hesitated . . . I could tell he was trying to decide whether it was a greater insult to leave me a quarter or to leave me nothing. Finally he decided on leaving the quarter. I took it.

You often get exceptionally good tips from people who have recently had either very good or very bad fortune. For some gamblers, part of the fun of hitting big is going out afterwards and spending ostentatiously at a bar, and they usually tip ostentatiously as well.

The other kind of good tipper—people who have had bad fortune—is harder to figure. Once I saw a marriage come apart, or so it seemed, right in front of me at the bar. Vicious accusations were traded, followed by a decision to separate, followed by an awful silence. Then the man got up, paid for the two beers, and put down a five-dollar bill. The woman looked at him with hatred, then reached in her purse and put down a five-dollar bill of her own. Then they both left.

The best tippers of all are people who work for tips themselves—waiters, waitresses, and other bartenders. People who have some money, but who have known poverty at some point in their lives, are usually good tippers. People who have had money all their lives are, in general, not good tippers. Sometimes obnoxious customers, when it comes time to pay the bill, will compensate for having given you a hard time by tipping well.

It is a good idea to give change in a way that makes it convenient for the customer to leave a tip. If a bill comes to $14.50, for instance, you should give the customer two quarters and five singles as change of a twenty-dollar bill, rather than two quarters and a five-dollar bill.

Some bartenders will keep their tips in a glass or dish that is in plain view on the back bar. This can work well as a reminder. If you leave your tips visible, however, you should not accumulate a pile of money that is so large that a customer might feel that his contribution is insignificant. If it is a good night, every once in a while take some money out of your dish and put it away in your pocket or purse.

21. Cash Register Technique

ON A BUSY NIGHT the clink of glasses, the conversation and laughter of the customers, and the music from the band or jukebox all add up to a kind of barroom concerto in which the solo instrument—especially in the viewpoint of management—is the bell of the cash register.

Even an experienced bartender, when starting a new job, will very likely have to be shown the peculiarities of the cash register, unless it is one he or she has worked with before. There are so many different brands and systems that it is not possible to give instructions that will apply completely to all of them. The orientation in this chapter will not take the place entirely of having the register explained to you when you start working. But it should give you a good head start in following that explanation.

Most of the older mechanical registers have a three-step system. The steps are:

1. Price
2. Type of item (beer, wine, food, previous balance, and so forth)
3. Type of transaction (charge, cash)

Let's suppose a customer orders a beer—a bottle of Miller—and gives you the money for it. You will be given a list of drink prices when you start, and you see from this that domestic beer in bottles is $1.25. So you ring:

1. 1.25
2. BEER
3. CASH

When you ring CASH, the drawer will pop open. You put the money for the beer in the drawer and, if necessary, make change.

Now let's suppose a couple comes in and they order a beer and a Gin and Tonic. They don't want to pay immediately, so you will run a tab for them. You write their order on a tab and stick it in the slot in the register. Usually there is some kind of marking on the slot to indicate where on the tab the register will print. Then you ring:

1.25
BEER
1.75
LIQUOR
CHARGE

The CHARGE key is called "service" in some systems, and is used to add items that have not yet been paid. The register will now print on the tab, and it will look something like this:

Miller   1.25 (B)
          1.75 (L)
G/T   3.00 (CH)

The $3.00 is not something you have rung, but an automatic total done by the machine when you press the CHARGE key.

Now let's suppose they order another round. You write "repeat" or something to that effect on the tab, and stick it in the slot again. This time you put it in a little lower, so that you don't overprint the prices above it. Then you ring:

3.00

PREVIOUS BALANCE

1.25

BEER

1.75

LIQUOR

CHARGE

And their tab will now look something like this:

Miller   1.25 (B)
G/T   1.75 (L)
         3.00 (CH)
repeat   3.00 (PB)
         1.25 (B)
         1.75 (L)
         6.00 (CH)

Then, after finishing their drinks, they ask for their tab. You fill in the amount by hand—$6.00 in this case—in the space at the bottom. You give them the tab, they give you the money, and you now ring:

6.00

PREVIOUS BALANCE

CASH

And the drawer pops open. The completed bill now looks like this:

Miller   1.25 (B)
G/T   1.75 (L)
         3.00 (CH)
repeat

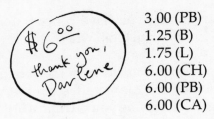

3.00 (PB)
1.25 (B)
1.75 (L)
6.00 (CH)
6.00 (PB)
6.00 (CA)

In the newer, computer-type registers, the chief difference is that you have a much greater number of keys for "type of item" and the price is usually entered automatically. In the older register, for instance, there was just one key for BEER, and the bartender had to enter the price. In the computer-type register, there will be a key for DRAFT, a key for BOTTLE, DOMESTIC, a key for BOTTLE, IMPORTED, and perhaps others. So if a man orders a bottle of Miller, and pays, there are only two steps:

BOTTLE, DOMESTIC
CASH

And the price appears automatically. This system makes it very easy for the bartender to learn the prices, and gives management a very detailed breakdown of the kinds of drinks being sold. With this kind of register, just about the only prices the bartender will ring will be for PREVIOUS BALANCE.

Sometimes state or local laws require you to collect tax. If you need to add tax to a bill, the mechanical registers have a SUBTOTAL key that you hit after you have rung all the items, but before you hit either CASH or CHARGE. After the register does the subtotal, you then consult the tax chart, which is usually right next to the register. Then you add tax as a separate item, and hit CASH or CHARGE. A bill with tax would read something like this:

Miller   1.25 (B)
G/T   1.75 (L)
          3.00 (SB)

.24 (T)
3.24 (CH)

On computer-type registers, when you hit the tax key the register will compute the amount automatically.

On both types of registers, there will be a CLEAR key. This will correct mis-rings if you catch them in time. On mechanical registers you can use this key to correct the price until you have hit the "type of item" key. On computer registers, you can usually use the CLEAR key until you have hit the "type of transaction" key. If it is too late to clear your mis-ring, then you must make out an over-ring slip. These are sometimes provided, and sometimes you will have to write them yourself, such as:

$1.25 Beer Over (CH)
Darlene

At the end of your shift, the bar manager will hit the BALANCE key on the register, and it will print out the totals for each category of sale—beer, wine, liquor, tax, and so on—and give the total for CASH. This amount, plus the amount that was in the drawer at the beginning of your shift, is the total amount of money that should now be in your drawer, after adjusting for mis-rings. You will be allowed a small margin for error, but if your drawer is often wrong by several dollars or more, this will be frowned upon.

You should keep the stacks of bills neat in the drawer, all facing up. Keep an eye on your supply of bills and change. If you are running low on anything, you should get more of what you need well in advance, and avoid the possibility of running out completely in the middle of a rush.

22. Alcoholism

SOME PEOPLE drink too much. If they do it habitually they are called alcoholics. It is now thought that who becomes an alcoholic and who does not is largely determined by our genes. There is no exact line separating the alcoholics from the heavy drinkers.

As a bartender, the great majority of the drinks you pour will be served to moderate, social drinkers. A certain number, however, will be served to people whose drinking has become self-destructive. As long as they are not drunk when they order, and not behaving in a way that is socially unacceptable, you must serve them. If you didn't, it wouldn't make the slightest difference to their condition. Alcoholics—believe me—do not stop drinking because someone refuses them a drink. Alcoholics stop drinking, if they ever do, because they lose their jobs, or their health

---

If you have one parent who is an alcoholic, your chances of becoming an alcoholic are 35 times higher than normal. If both parents are alcoholics, your chances are 400 times higher than normal.

—DAVID SMITH, M.D.

---

falls apart, or their family or social life falls apart, or some combination of these things.

The alcoholic makes a trade. He trades his health, sometimes his job, sometimes his family, sometimes his self-respect, in return for the pleasure of drinking. In some cases, this pleasure seems a poor thing—only a dulling of the mind, and, with it, a dulling of anxiety. There are others, though, who have what you might almost call a genius—or at least a talent—for drunkenness. Alcohol frees their minds from certain restrictions and allows them to take off on flights of madness, euphoria, and laughter. I have known—and loved—many people like this. They can be enormously charming and funny as casual acquaintances, but they usually cause great pain to those close to them.

Is the trade worth it? For most people it isn't, fortunately. The alcoholic, however, says that it is worth it—with actions if not words. When the trade no longer seems worth it, he or she will consult a doctor, or a clergyman, or Alcoholics Anonymous. While he is still willing to make the trade, he will consult his bartender.

Once an alcoholic's drinking has reached a certain point, it is impossible for him or her to cut down and become a normal, social drinker. He must either quit completely or continue to drink self-destructively. It is very difficult for alcoholics to face this fact, and it is very common for them to kid themselves—"I can cut down any time I want to."

It is always useless to talk to an alcoholic about his drinking when he is drunk.

Many older alcoholics acquire monstrous purple noses. This is because a high blood-alcohol level causes red blood cells to clump together. These clumps get stuck in the small blood vessels of the nose and cause them to burst. The same thing happens in the small blood vessels of the brain, and, as a result, many veteran alcoholics are slightly childish and fuzzy-minded, even when they are sober. Over a period of time, alcohol can also damage the heart, the liver, and the digestive system. It lowers the body's resistance to infection, and can lead to malnutrition if it reaches the point where the alcoholic stops eating.

Alcoholics Anonymous—"A.A."—is a volunteer organization of recovered alcoholics that helps new members to stop drinking. There are chapters all over the country, and they are listed in the phone book.

23. Bartending and the Law

MOST OF THE LAWS that concern bartenders are state laws, and many may vary slightly from one state to another. If you have any questions about the specific laws in your state, you can consult the state liquor commission or your attorney. There are some general practices, however, that apply in almost every state.

In every state there is a state liquor commission, or alcoholic beverage control office, as it is sometimes called, that issues licenses and establishes regulations. This office may require bartenders to be licensed by them. The state liquor commission may have inspectors of its own, with the authority to levy fines, but usually these inspectors do not have the authority to make arrests. This is done by the state or local police, who in fact are the principal enforcers of most of the liquor laws.

In most states, the driver of a motor vehicle is considered to be impaired when the blood/alcohol level is over .10 percent (This means one-tenth of one percent, and not ten percent.) One drink in this chart = one ounce of 100° liquor = 12 ounces of beer = 4 ounces of table wine. Subtract .01 for each hour of drinking.

BLOOD/ALCOHOL PERCENTAGE

Drinks	Body Weight In Pounds								Effect
	100	120	140	160	180	200	220	240	
1	.04	.03	.03	.02	.02	.02	.02	.02	Rarely
2	.08	.06	.05	.05	.04	.04	.03	.03	Impaired
3	.11	.09	.08	.07	.06	.06	.05	.05	
4	.15	.12	.11	.09	.08	.08	.07	.06	Possibly
5	.19	.16	.13	.12	.11	.09	.09	.08	Impaired
6	.23	.19	.16	.14	.13	.11	.10	.09	
7	.26	.22	.19	.16	.15	.13	.12	.11	
8	.30	.25	.21	.19	.17	.15	.14	.13	Definitely
9	.34	.28	.24	.21	.19	.17	.15	.14	Impaired
10	.38	.31	.27	.23	.21	.19	.17	.16	

The three most important legal prohibitions for bartenders are:

1. You must not serve anyone after legal closing, or before legal opening
2. You must not serve minors.
3. You must not serve intoxicated people.

The legal drinking age will vary from state to state, and the permitted hours of operation will vary, but all states that permit liquor to be sold by the drink have these laws in some form.

There are usually criminal penalties for breaking any of these laws. In other words, you could be fined and/or go to jail. Enforcement of the criminal penalties, of course, depends on local practices and on circumstances. In a bar that is known to have a very young clientele, for instance, the police may come around frequently to check for underage drinkers. In a bar with a predominantly mature clientele, they may never check for this at all. Even in the latter case, though, the bartender still needs to be careful. If there is only one underage drinker in a crowded bar, and that drinker should later go out and kill someone in a car wreck, the bartender could very well face criminal charges.

If you are making drinks that are served by a cocktail waitress or waiter, that does not necessarily let you off the hook if those drinks are served to intoxicated people. If the bar is so large that you cannot see the people to whom the drinks are being served, then you most likely cannot be held liable. In a smaller place, it is conceivable that you and the server of the drinks could be held jointly responsible.

What is perhaps more frightening than the thought of criminal prosecution is the possibility of a civil suit brought by someone who claims he was injured as a result of a drink that you poured. You "expose yourself to liability for negligence," as the lawyers say, when you serve someone who is intoxicated. If a man orders a drink from you, then falls and breaks his arm on the way home, he probably cannot hold you legally responsible for his injuries. If a third party is injured, however, the legal danger to the bartender becomes quite real. So if you serve a person seventeen Bloody Marys, and that person then goes out and causes an automobile collision that leaves a famous ballerina as a paraplegic, your financial liability—not to mention your moral guilt—will be staggering. And the owner of the bar would share this liability.

Cases of this kind either go to juries, or are settled out of court on the basis of what lawyers and insurance companies think would happen if they did go to juries. The jury will be instructed to decide whether an average, reasonable person, in the position of the bartender in question, would have been able to tell that the customer in question was intoxicated. There is no exact number of drinks or blood alcohol that would determine the guilt of the bartender in a case like this. In most states, drivers are presumed by the police to be drunk if their blood alcohol level is one-tenth (.1) of one percent or more. A jury may be convinced, however, that the bartender had no reasonable way of knowing the customer was intoxicated, even though his blood alcohol level was later found to be, say, .11 or .12 percent. This would be especially true if it were a busy night and the customer had been drinking someplace else, and just came to your bar for his last one or two drinks.

If a customer of yours should ever be involved in some situation like this, remember that *silence is golden*. A police officer, for instance, may come to question you about an auto accident involving a customer who was last served by you. You should answer all innocent questions, such as, "Were you working last night?" and "Do you know Joe Doyle?" But if there is any chance that the customer left your bar in a state that might be open to question, you should not answer any questions such as, "Did he have a lot to drink last night?" or "How long was he in here?" You can say something like, "I think you'd better talk to my boss about that," or, if pressed, "I'm sorry, officer, but for reasons of privacy and other reasons, I make it a rule never to discuss the drinking habits of my patrons." The police officer may only be conducting a routine investigation into a traffic accident, with no thought of bringing charges against you. Nevertheless, if at some point a civil suit is brought against you and the bar, the officer can be called as a witness—and everything you said to him, and which he wrote in his notebook, can be used as evidence.

Above all, don't lie to the police. If a man had six Gin and Tonics, don't say he had two or three. If there were to be a trial, his tab could be subpoenaed, or there could be witnesses, and right off the bat it would be established that you are a liar.

By no means do I believe that a bartender should serve people irresponsibly, and then try to evade the consequences. I do believe, however, that justice is not always on the side of the person bringing the suit, and I think the bartender should know enough not to set himself up.

24. Bartender Jokes

THE BEST BARTENDER JOKES are not the memorized ones, but those that pop up in the cross-bar banter that flows every night in bars around the world. It's difficult to write down this kind of humor, because it is so much a part of a particular moment, and depends on the time of night and the particular personalities involved.

I used to go to a bar in New York that was tended by a morose, pear-shaped Englishman named Dudley. Dudley was a man of few words, but when he did speak he was very funny. One night a woman I was with said to him, "Dudley, don't you ever smile?"

"Delivering the sacrament is no joke, my dear," he replied.

Occasionally you can find an opening for the old standby, the Pine Float. For example:

"Hey, Mary Beth, how's about a drink on the house?"

"Well, I guess I could let you have a Pine Float."

"A Pine Float? What's that?"

"A toothpick in a glass of water! Hahahahaaaa!"

Women bartenders handle rude remarks from male customers in different ways. I once worked with a very attractive woman bartender named Pat. She always behaved with perfect correctness, but when a man would make a gross remark to her, she had a talent for coming back with something twice as gross that would drop him in his tracks. Once someone said to her, "Pat, I'd give a hundred dollars to get in your pants." "What's the matter," she answered, "did you shit in yours?"

Some bartenders have a talent for memorizing and telling jokes. They hear them from customers and repeat them to other customers, forming an important part of the network that distributes new jokes. Many of these are off-color, to say the least. Here are some of the more printable ones I have heard lately.

*

A man walks into a bar with a pig. The pig is wearing sunglasses, and has a towel around its neck. The man orders a beer for himself and a Seven and Seven for the pig.

"Where'd you get the pig, Lou?" asks the bartender.

"Well, I was driving home one night," says the man, "and it fell out of the back of a pickup truck right in front of me. The truck kept on going, so I stopped and picked it up, but now I don't know what to do with it. It's getting to be kind of a nuisance."

"Why don't you take it to the zoo?" asks the bartender.

"I did, but today it wants to go to the beach."

*

One of the regulars at a certain night club was a man with a wooden eye. He felt very self-conscious about his condition, and spent most nights quietly drinking by himself. One Saturday night there was dancing at the night club, and the man remained at the bar drinking, ignoring the crowd and the music. Then he noticed, sitting across the room, a woman who was also drinking alone. She had a kind of orange fungus growing on one side of her face. "That might be the woman for me," thought the man. "Maybe we could get it on. I'll go ask her to dance!" So he went up to her and said, "Excuse me, but would you like to dance?"

"Would I? Would I!" cried the woman.

"Skin condition! Skin condition!" said the man.

*

A mathematician, an architect, and a lawyer are sitting in a rural tavern, bragging about their dogs. The mathematician says to the other two, "Just let me show you guys something. Hypotenuse! Come over here. Now, how much is two and three?"

"Arf! Arf! Arf! Arf! Arf!" answers Hypotenuse.

"That was nothing," says the architect. "Frank Lloyd! Come over here," he says to his dog. "Now, boy, build me a structure!" And the dog builds a small model of the Eiffel Tower out of cocktail stirrers.

Next it is the lawyer's turn. "Okay, Plaintiff," says the lawyer to his dog, "Show them what you can do!" And the lawyer's dog screws the other two dogs and takes the rest of the afternoon off.

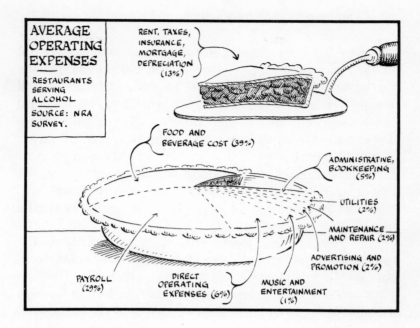

AVERAGE OPERATING EXPENSES

RESTAURANTS SERVING ALCOHOL

SOURCE: NRA SURVEY.

RENT, TAXES, INSURANCE, MORTGAGE, DEPRECIATION (13%)

FOOD AND BEVERAGE COST (39%)

ADMINISTRATIVE, BOOKKEEPING (5%)

UTILITIES (2%)

MAINTENANCE AND REPAIR (2%)

ADVERTISING AND PROMOTION (2%)

PAYROLL (29%)

DIRECT OPERATING EXPENSES (6%)

MUSIC AND ENTERTAINMENT (1%)

25. Bar Management

L IKE MOST THINGS in a bar or restaurant, bar policies reflect the temperament and philosophy of the owner or the general manager. These policies can be highly system-atized, involving lots of paperwork, or they can be in-formal, and based on personal relationships with em-ployees. Either way can work—at least in a fairly small establishment—and either way can fail. Bar management can be overdone and can also be underdone. Overdone, bar management can result in an unprofitable amount of time spent in trying to account for every last drop of liquor, and every last maraschino cherry, creating a police-state atmosphere that antagonizes the staff and has counterproductive results. But if there is little or no management, profits can be hemorrhaged away through theft and sloppiness.

In a small operation, the bar manager is often the owner. In a larger place, one of the bartenders will be designated the head bartender. The head bartender will usually get first choice of hours to work tending bar, and will be responsible for such things as hiring and firing, keeping track of inventory, and ordering. In a still larger place, the bar manager will work full time at managing.

If all drinks came in individual bottles, like beer, the job of the bar manager would be greatly simplified. Problems arise because drinks must be portioned out of the bottle by the bartenders.

There can be no effective bar management unless the amount of liquor poured in each drink is standardized. There are a few ways in which this can be done. The best ways of controlling pouring are to have the bartenders use shot glasses to measure all their drinks, or to install the kind of pourers on all bottles that automatically pour a predetermined amount. Both of these methods are very good for establishing portion control, but they also have drawbacks. They slow the bartender down, for one thing, so that the increase in labor cost can to some extent offset the savings in liquor. The automatic pourers often get clogged, especially those used on the sweet liquors, and they make it difficult to pour the odd amounts called for in certain recipes. The biggest drawback to both these systems, though, is that in many parts of the country they run against the grain of local custom. At a bar at a major airport, or in a large hotel chain, these systems may be appropriate. But in a more local market, if free pouring is the accepted practice then use of the shot glass or the automatic pourers can be resented by the clientele and give an impression that is somewhat tightfisted and unfriendly. Bartenders also dislike these systems.

It is possible to have control with a free-pouring system, but it requires a little extra training and watchfulness on the part of management. If you have a free-pouring policy, it is a good idea to have all new employees use a measuring glass for the first few weeks, so that they have a clear idea of the amount they are supposed to pour. It is also a good idea to use small rocks glasses, so that when they are packed with ice it's impossible to overpour by very much. Every once in a while the bar manager should spot check the pouring in rocks drinks by straining the ice from a drink that has just been poured, and measuring the drink in a shot glass. If the drink has been overpoured or underpoured significantly, it should be called to the bartender's attention. A free-pouring system can work amazingly well if employees are clearly aware of their responsibilities, and if there is proper supervision. A free-pouring system that simply abandons control, however, can be a disaster.

Once a standard size for drinks has been established, the average liquor cost per drink can be determined. If it is decided to pour 1½-ounce drinks, for instance, each quart will yield about 21 drinks (32 ÷ 1.5 = 21). Then, if the average bottle of bar liquor cost $6.50, the liquor cost of the average bar drink will be $6.50 divided by 21, or approximately $.31. Now the selling price of the drink can be established. For a liquor cost that will be, say, 20 percent of the selling price, your selling price should be $.31 times five, or $1.55. This can be rounded off to $1.50 or $1.75. Or it might be decided that two-ounce drinks for $2.00 would be more attractive to customers. The liquor cost is still 20 percent. After the price for bar drinks is established, the same procedure can be used for call drinks, for top shelf drinks, and for drinks calling for more than the usual amount of liquor.

The 20 percent figure used above should not be taken as any kind of industry-wide standard. The percentage needed to make a profit will vary from one place to another, depending on volume of business and overhead expenses. And prices, of course, must be competitive. Once you have determined the percentage that is appropriate for your operation, it can be used as an indication of how well the control system is working. So if your cash register shows that you have sold $1,000 in liquor in a given period, and if your liquor cost has been established to be 20 percent, you should need to order approximately $200 worth of liquor to replace what was used in that period. Costs significantly above that probably indicate that someone has developed a heavy hand in pouring, or there has been theft. Or it may just be that liquor prices have gone up, and it is time to adjust your selling prices.

Taking inventory of the liquor stock is a task that has to be done periodically, usually weekly or biweekly. Inventory sheets usually look something like this:

	Bar Stock	Under-bar Stock	Service Bar	Stock Room	Total
Bar Vodka					
Smirnoff					
Smirnoff 100°					
Stolichnaya					
Absolut					
Bar Gin					
Beefeater					
Tanqueray					
↓					
etc.					

For convenience, bottles in the stock room should be kept in the same order as on the inventory sheets. Open bottles in the bar are estimated, usually to the nearest quarter. The inventory sheets give management another form of control over liquor stock, and they are also used as a way of telling what needs to be ordered.

Ordering liquor and taking care of the necessary paperwork is another responsibility of the bar manager.

Enough liquor must be ordered so that the bar never runs out of the essentials, but money should not be tied up uselessly in inventory. You may be offered a great bargain if you buy a whole case of ouzo. If it takes two and a half years to use up that case of ouzo, however, it is a false economy. That money could have been working for the bar somehow, instead of sitting on the shelves of the stock room. The bar manager should make sure that all deliveries are checked against the accompanying invoice, so that the bar actually gets what it is paying for.

The stock room in which the liquor is kept should be locked, and access to that room should be limited to as few employees as is practical. When a bartender needs to restock from the liquor room, a requisition slip should be filled out. This is a list of how many bottles of what kinds of liquors were taken, with the employee's signature. Normally, these requisition slips need not be checked against the weekly inventory, but they give the employees the idea that things are being accounted for, and that they are responsible for what they take. And if there is a problem with disappearing liquor, the requisition slips are available to help track down the problem.

There must also be some controls on the handling of cash in the bar. For a start, there should be a rule that every sale should be rung immediately. In the case of a cash sale, the money should be rung into the register. If the customer wants to run a tab, the tab should be written and rung immediately. Otherwise, a customer can sit at the bar for half an hour drinking a beer, and then get up and leave a dollar on the bar. By that time, even the bartender may not remember if the dollar is in payment for the beer, or if it is a tip.

There should also be control over complimentary drinks. People enjoy getting something for nothing, and drinkers are certainly no exception to this. Complimentary drinks can be a very effective promotional device. A free drink gives a customer the feeling that he is well liked and somehow special, and this can be a bond that will bring him back. If a bartender is given carte blanche to give out complimentary drinks, however, there is a great temptation to overdo it. The interests of the bartender, after all, are different from those of the management. The bartender is very likely to increase his tips and popularity by giving free drinks, but he doesn't have to worry about the cost of the liquor, as does management.

If someone from management is usually in the bar, that person should probably have the exclusive authority to order complimentary drinks for customers. A bartender who has to work unsupervised much of the time may be given this privilege under very clearly limited circumstances. Every complimentary drink given by the bartender should be listed on a "promo sheet," and there should be a maximum number established for any one night. The promo sheet, besides acting as a form of control, is also necessary as a record, so these drinks can be deducted as an operating expense.

As a bartender, your job is to follow the established procedures of bar policy where you work. As a bar manager, your job is to constantly examine these procedures to see how they might be improved. Should the Daiquiris be made with fresh limes rather than a pre-mix? Should you install video games? What can you do to attract more customers? What kind of customers are you trying to attract? Should you develop and promote some special house drinks? You should constantly be looking for ways to make the bar a better and more profitable operation.

Another function of the bar manager is to tell the bartenders when they are doing something wrong, or right. A good rule for this is the adage, *Praise in public, blame in private.* In the bar business, you are often dealing with damaged egos to begin with. If someone is not doing the job, he or she must be spoken to, but it should be done with some restraint. The staff should be passing on positive feelings to the customers, and they will not be able to do this if they are needlessly made to feel humiliated and resentful.

> I NEVER WORKED FOR ANYBODY IN MY LIFE. THEY MIGHT HAVE **THOUGHT** I WAS WORKING FOR THEM, BUT THEY WERE WORKING FOR **ME!**

26. How to Get a Job

IN THE YELLOW PAGES there are more pages under "Restaurants" than almost any other section. Add to this the listings for "Night Clubs" and you see that the whole food service industry—which includes bars—is enormous. In most of these places, the demand for new employees is fairly constant. Once in a while you will hear of a person who has spent ten years, or twenty years, or a lifetime, as a bartender, but they are exceptions. Most bartenders stay bartenders for a relatively short time, and then move on to some other kind of work. For those who stay longer, it's very common to move from one bar or restaurant to another. In many areas, the bar and restaurant business increases seasonally, and new bartenders have to be hired every year at the beginning of the season. So the jobs are out there.

Once you get your first bartending job, you will not have much trouble getting others. Getting the first job, however, may require some extra effort because, everything else being equal, employers prefer hiring experienced workers. Keep trying. Don't be discouraged if you apply for two or three jobs and don't get hired. You may have to apply for two or three *dozen.*

Begin with the help-wanted ads in the newspaper. Get the paper as soon as it comes out, and call the bar or restaurant as soon as possible. Ask when would be a convenient time to come for an interview. If the ad says "apply in person," don't go during periods of peak business. Just after opening is usually a good time, or in the middle of the afternoon.

After exhausting the help-wanted ads, just go around to bars and restaurants where you think you'd like to work. Tell them you're a bartender looking for a job, and ask if anything is available. In a high-turnover field like bartending, this approach often pays off. If you come at the right time, and make a good impression, you may be hired on the spot, to save the trouble of placing an ad in the paper and conducting time-consuming interviews. In areas with seasonal business, try making the rounds about six weeks or so before the beginning of the season.

When you go job hunting, your clothing and personal grooming—hair, fingernails, and so forth—should be immaculate. You will probably be given an application form to fill out first. In the space for "Trade or Vocational School" you can put "Buller's Professional Course in Bartending." If you have any previous restaurant or bar experience, put that down, too; it will be in your favor.

After the application form comes the interview. The interviewer will probably want to find out more about your work history, and about what kind of a person you are in general. He or she will be looking for someone who has a good appearance, who seems honest, and who communicates well.

If you are the kind of person who is scrupulously honest in even the smallest details of your personal life, I would certainly not want to counsel you to be dishonest in any way in trying to get a job. You should know, however, that many bartenders get their first job by exaggerating their work experience. What they do is to pick a restaurant or bar that is defunct, or in another state, and claim that they worked there for a short time as a bartender. They don't want to claim to be a seasoned veteran, because it will later become obvious to someone who knows the business that this is not so. They claim just a little experience, which they hope may be enough to elevate their application above those with no experience at all.

If you are reasonably sharp and you know the material in this book, including the thirty basic cocktails, you should be able to pull something like this off. When you get behind the bar, you will have to learn where each liquor is kept, and it will take practice to get used to the register. But even an experienced bartender takes a few days to get used to a new bar, especially if it is set up differently from what he is used to and has a different type of register. After observing you for a while, management may very well suspect that your experience was exaggerated, if not totally fabricated, but if you seem to know the basic drinks, and seem willing and capable, you probably won't be fired.

As a rule new bartenders, experienced or not, are not asked to start work in the middle of a busy night. They are usually started on slow nights, or afternoons, under the guidance of a more experienced bartender. Naturally you will want to take full advantage of this training period to learn as much as you can. It might even be a good idea to spend a few hours in the bar sometime before you start, observing how things are done and perhaps asking the bartender a few questions about the procedures at that particular bar. If you do this, drink only juice or soda.

In spite of federal and, in some cases, state laws, discrimination because of sex, age, and race is very common in the hiring of bartenders. What makes this discrimination perhaps a little less objectionable than discrimination in other fields is that it is not directed solely against any one group. Bars with a young clientele, for instance, may prefer to have bartenders of the same age group. The same may be true, however, for bars with an older clientele. There are bars that prefer to hire attractive young women as bartenders, and there are bars that feel that men fit in better with the image they are trying to project. When you go into a bar and see only members of the opposite sex working there, you shouldn't automatically give up on making an application. It may be just a coincidence, or it may be that they prefer, say, women in the evenings and men for weekend afternoons. On the other hand, when you are making the rounds looking for work, you should at least be aware of this consideration, and ask yourself at which type of bar you might best fit in.

You should also ask yourself at which type of bar you would most enjoy working. If you like to tell jokes and discuss sports, you will probably not be happy working at the bar of an expensive formal restaurant. If you are reserved and aristocratic, you will probably not last long at the kind of bar that usually has several motorcycles parked out front.

If all else fails, take a job as a waiter or a waitress at a restaurant, with the understanding that you will move into the bar when there is an opening. These jobs are easier to come by than bartending jobs, and the experience will be helpful to you as a bartender.

27. Tricks of the Trade

YOU CAN LIFT six glasses at once if each finger holds an outside glass, and the pressure from these glasses holds the one in the center (see illustration). This only works with glasses that are the same size.

*

If you anticipate a very busy night, do as much work as you can in advance. You can prepare a few Old Fashioned set-ups by putting the fruit, sugar, and bitters in the bottom of the glass. Then, when you get an order for one, all you have to do is add the soda, ice, and whiskey. You can also pre-pour a few carafes of wine.

*

For an upset stomach, a good remedy is a teaspoon or so of Angostura bitters in a small glass of club soda or ginger ale. Bitters contain an extract of gentian root, which has been used in herbal medicine to treat digestive problems since the time of the ancient Greeks.

*

A hangover remedy that I have found to work if taken *before* I start drinking is the Megavitamin Prairie Oyster:

> 1,000 mg. vitamin B_1
> 1,000 mg. vitamin C
> 1,000 mg. L-cystene

This has its limits, of course. The reader should also be warned that the Megavitamin Prairie Oyster is still considered experimental, and that the author of this book is a bartender and not a physician.

*

Keep a Band-Aid in your wallet or purse.

"spiralling" cocktail napkins makes them easier to pick up one at a time

*

You will frequently be asked by customers for a pen and a piece of scrap paper that they can use. Keep these available.

*

Whenever possible, always give a hand to fellow workers—waitresses, waiters, dishwashers, maitre d'— even if it is "not your job." You will find that this help will come back to you when you need it.

*

Try to minimize the number of trips you make back and forth along the bar. If you have to travel all the way to the other end of the bar for some reason, ask yourself if there is something else you can do or get while you are there, to save yourself from making another trip.

*

Whenever possible, try to learn to work with two hands instead of just one.

*

When passing other employees, keep to the right.

*

Don't get drunk on the job, don't steal, and don't give out free drinks, except possibly to the author of this book. Good luck!

Drink Reference
Section

NEW DRINKS, like new songs, are constantly coming into being. Most of them are flops. A few might have a year or two of popularity in a limited area, and then sink into obscurity. A very few will endure and become old standards. In the following list I have tried to include only old standards and current favorites. I will leave it to other books to record for posterity the Edsels of mixology.

The amounts in the following recipes may have to be adjusted to fit the pouring policies of the bar where you are working. The recipe for a Screwdriver given here, for instance, call for 1½ ounces of vodka, but you will find some bars that pour 1-ounce highballs, and some that pour 2 ounces. There is no absolute standard.

You will also have to adapt new recipes to established pouring policies. After tending bar for a while, you will come to know most of the old standards, and most of the currently popular regional favorites. Beyond this point, most of the drinks you will learn will be newly created ones. A customer will come up to the bar and say, "Do you know how to make a Green Meanie?"

"No," you will answer, "but I'll be glad to if you can tell me the ingredients." Sometimes the customer will not know either, in which case you can sometimes get the recipe from another bartender: "Hey, Lori, do you know what goes in a Green Meanie?" "Sure, it's Midori, Southern Comfort, and pineapple juice." This is usually how bartenders will communicate recipes—not using precise measurements, but just the basic ingredients. You will then substitute these ingredients for those of a drink whose recipe and price has already been established. In this case, the best drink to use as a model would be the Singapore Sling.

The recipes below should be used as general guides, but exact proportions can be varied to suit a customer's taste or your own. A Rusty Nail, for example, is usually made with less Drambuie than scotch. If you know a customer likes sweet drinks, however, you might make it almost half and half. There are also optional modifiers that can be added in small amounts to subtly accent the flavor of some drinks, like herbs in cooking. A few drops of bitters in a Manhattan would be an example of this, or a few drops of Benedictine on top of a Singapore Sling.

Keep in mind that some drinks will evolve over a period of time. Today's Martini drinker would not even recognize the original version of this drink (see page 14). After a hundred years, five ingredients have been reduced to two, and the proportions of those two completely reversed.

To complicate things further, you will find that some drinks go by more than one name, and that some names are attached to more than one drink. In the latter case, you must check to find out which version the customer wants.

Alabama Slammer (build)

1 ounce Southern Comfort
1 ounce sloe gin
Fill with orange juice.
GLASS: Collins, with ice
FRUIT: orange slice

Americano (build)

1 ounce Campari
1 ounce sweet vermouth
GLASS: rocks, with ice
FRUIT: twist

Angel's Tit (build)

1 ounce dark crème de cacao
Top with whipped cream.
GLASS: pony
FRUIT: cherry on top

B-52 (build)

1 part Tia Maria
1 part Irish cream liqueur
1 part Grand Marnier
Float Irish cream on Tia Maria, and Grand Marnier on Irish
    cream.
GLASS: pony

Bacardi Cocktail (shake)

*A Daiquiri made with Bacardi rum, and with a splash of grenadine
    syrup.*

1½ ounces Bacardi rum
1 ounce lime mix
GLASS: cocktail
FRUIT: lime wedge

Between the Sheets (shake)

½ ounce brandy
½ ounce rum
½ ounce triple sec
1 ounce lemon mix
GLASS: cocktail

Black Russian (build)

1 ounce vodka
1 ounce coffee liqueur
GLASS: rocks, with ice

Bloody Mary (shake)

1½ ounces vodka
½ ounce Rose's Lime Juice
4 dashes worcestershire sauce
1 dash tabasco
Salt and pepper
Fill with tomato juice and shake lightly.
GLASS: Collins, with ice
FRUIT: celery stalk

Bloody Maria (shake)
*A Bloody Mary made with tequila instead of vodka, and
    usually with some extra tabasco.*

Blue Blazer

2 ounces heated scotch
2 ounces boiling water
1 teaspoon sugar

In a heated mug, place sugar and water.
In a second heated mug, place scotch, and set aflame.
Pour ingredients back and forth several times, with much
    showmanship.
When flame is extinguished, pour into warmed wine glass.
Garnish with twist.

Blue Blazer #2 (build)

¾ ounce peppermint schnapps
¾ ounce Southern Comfort
Float the Southern Comfort on the schnapps.
Ignite, and serve aflame.
GLASS: shot

Blue Moon (blend)

1 ounce rum
1 ounce blue curaçao
1 tablespoon coconut syrup
Pineapple juice
Scoop of ice
GLASS: brandy snifter or specialty glass
FRUIT: orange slice
(For history, see p. 29)

Bocci Ball (build)
An amaretto Screwdriver.

1½ ounces amaretto
Fill with orange juice.
GLASS: highball, with ice

Boilermaker

1½ ounces whiskey in a shot glass, with a beer chaser.

Brandied Port (stir)

1 ounce port
1 ounce brandy
½ ounce sweet vermouth
GLASS: cocktail
FRUIT: twist

Brandy Alexander (shake)

¾ ounce brandy
¾ ounce dark crème de cacao
1 ounce cream (or milk)
GLASS: champagne
GARNISH: powdered nutmeg

Brandy Cass (shake)

1½ ounces brandy
½ ounce crème de cassis
½ ounce lemon mix
GLASS: cocktail

Brave Bull (build)

1 ounce tequila
1 ounce coffee liqueur
GLASS: rocks, with ice

Bronx (shake)

1 ounce gin
½ ounce dry vermouth
½ ounce sweet vermouth
½ ounce orange juice
GLASS: cocktail
FRUIT: orange slice

Bull Shot (build)

1½ ounces vodka
Fill with beef bouillon.
GLASS: rocks, with ice

California Root Beer (build)

1 ounce Galliano
1 ounce coffee liqueur
Fill with cola.
GLASS: Collins, with ice

California Root Beer Float (build)

1 ounce Galliano
1 ounce coffee liqueur
Fill with cola.
Add splash of milk.
GLASS: Collins, with ice

Cape Cod (build)
A Screwdriver made with cranberry instead of orange juice.

1½ ounces vodka
Fill with sweetened cranberry juice.
GLASS: highball, with ice

Champagne Cocktail (build)

Mix ½ teaspoon sugar and dash of Angostura
bitters in champagne glass.
Add chilled champagne.
GLASS: champagne
FRUIT: twist

Champerelle (build)

1 part orange curaçao
1 part anisette
1 part Green Chartreuse
1 part cognac
Float in layers, with curaçao on the bottom and cognac on
    top.
GLASS: pony

Chi Chi (blend)
A Pina Colada made with vodka instead of rum.

2 ounces vodka
1 tablespoon coconut syrup
Pineapple juice
Ice
GLASS: brandy snifter or specialty glass
GARNISH: pineapple stick or cherry

Colorado M—f— (shake)
A Dirty Mother with cola.

1 ounce tequila
1 ounce coffee liqueur
Fill with milk; shake; add splash of cola.
GLASS: Collins

Coup de Cafard (stir)

1 ounce gin
½ ounce cognac
½ ounce sweet vermouth
¼ ounce orange curaçao
¼ ounce port
Dash of Angostura bitters
GLASS: cocktail

Creamsicle (shake)

1 ounce vodka
1 ounce triple sec
Fill with half milk, half orange juice.
GLASS: Collins, with ice

Crème de Menthe Frappé (build)

1½ ounces green crème de menthe
GLASS: rocks, with shaved ice

Cuba Libre (build)
A Rum and Coke with lime.

1½ ounces rum
Fill with cola.
GLASS: highball, with ice
FRUIT: couple of lime wedges

Cuban Screw (build)

A Screwdriver with rum instead of vodka.

1½ ounces rum
Fill with orange juice.
GLASS: highball, with ice

 Daiquiri (shake)

1½ ounces rum
1 ounce lime mix
GLASS: cocktail
FRUIT: lime wedge
(For history, see p. 44)

Dirty Mother (shake)

1 ounce tequila
1 ounce coffee liqueur
Fill with milk and shake.
GLASS: Collins, with ice

DuBarry (stir)

1½ ounces gin
½ ounce dry vermouth
½ ounce Pernod
Dash Angostura bitters
GLASS: cocktail
FRUIT: orange slice

Dubonnet Cocktail (stir)

1½ ounces gin
1 ounce red Dubonnet
GLASS: cocktail
FRUIT: twist

Fish House Punch (build)

1 ounce rum
½ ounce brandy
½ ounce peach brandy
Fill with lemon mix and add a squirt of cola.
GLASS: Collins

Floridita Daiquiri (blend)

1½ ounces rum
Dash of maraschino liqueur (or cherry brandy)
½ ounce Rose's Lime Juice
½ ounce grapefruit juice
Scoop of ice
GLASS: wine or large cocktail

Flying Grasshopper (stir)

1 ounce vodka
¾ ounce green crème de menthe
¾ ounce white crème de cacao
GLASS: cocktail

Freddie Fudpucker (build)
A Harvey Wallbanger made with tequila instead of vodka.

1½ ounces tequila
Fill with orange juice.
Float ½ ounce Galliano on top.
GLASS: highball, with ice

French Connection (build)

1½ ounces cognac
½ ounce amaretto
GLASS: rocks, with ice

French 75 (build)

1½ ounces brandy
1 ounce lemon mix
Fill with champagne.
GLASS: Collins, with ice
FRUIT: cherry

Frozen Banana Daiquiri (blend)

2 ounces banana liqueur
Half a banana
Lime mix to fill
Ice
GLASS: snifter or specialty glass

Frozen Strawberry Daiquiri (blend)

2 ounces strawberry liqueur
¼ cup strawberries
Lime mix
Ice
GLASS: snifter or specialty glass
FRUIT: lime

Gibson (stir)
A Martini that is garnished with a cocktail onion instead of an olive.

2 ounces gin
½ ounce dry vermouth
GLASS: cocktail
FRUIT: onion

Gimlet, Gin (stir)

2 ounces gin
½ ounce Rose's Lime Juice
GLASS: cocktail
FRUIT: lime

Gimlet, Vodka (stir)

2 ounces vodka
½ ounce Rose's Lime Juice
GLASS: cocktail
FRUIT: lime wedge

Gin and It (build)
Not chilled.

2 ounces gin
1 ounce sweet vermouth
GLASS: cocktail

Gin Cassis (shake)

1½ ounces gin
½ ounce crème de cassis
½ ounce lemon mix
GLASS: cocktail

Gin Rickey (build)

1½ ounces gin
Fill with club soda.
GLASS: highball, with ice
FRUIT: lime

Glögg

A Scandinavian wine punch, pronounced "glook."

1 liter port
1 liter sherry
Pour into a kettle.
Add a cheesecloth spicebag containing:
    2 ounces dried orange peel
    20 cardamom seeds
    20 cloves
Simmer for 15 minutes, then add:
    1 pound blanched almonds
    1 pound seedless raisins
Remove from heat.
Place wire grill over top of kettle, and place a pound of sugar
    cubes on the grill.
Pour a liter of brandy over the sugar cubes and light them.
When sugar has melted, extinguish the flame with the lid of
    the kettle.
Ladle into punch cups, along with the almonds and raisins.

Glüh Wein

A hot wine punch, pronounced "glue vine."

8 ounces red wine
1 teaspoon sugar
1 clove
1 strip orange peel
1 strip lemon peel
1 cinnamon stick
Heat in a saucepan, without boiling.
Strain into highball glass.

Godfather (build)

1½ ounces scotch
½ ounce amaretto
GLASS: rocks, with ice

Godmother (build)

1½ ounces vodka
½ ounce amaretto
GLASS: rocks, with ice

Golden Cadillac (shake)

1 ounce Galliano
½ ounce white crème de cacao
1 ounce cream (or milk)
GLASS: champagne

Golden Dream (shake)

1 ounce Galliano
½ ounce triple sec
½ ounce orange juice
1 ounce cream
GLASS: champagne
FRUIT: orange slice

Good and Plenty (build)

1 ounce ouzo
1 ounce amaretto
GLASS: rocks, with ice

 Grasshopper (shake)

¾ ounce green crème de menthe
¾ ounce white crème de cacao
1 ounce cream (or milk)
GLASS: champagne

Green Meanie (build)

1 ounce Midori
1 ounce Southern Comfort
Fill with pineapple juice.
GLASS: Collins, with ice

Greyhound (build)

1½ ounces vodka
Fill with grapefruit juice.
GLASS: rocks, with ice

 Harvey Wallbanger (build)
A Screwdriver with Galliano on top.

1½ ounces vodka
Fill with orange juice.
Float ½ ounce Galliano on top.
GLASS: highball, with ice

Hawaiian Punch (shake)

1 ounce sloe gin
¾ ounce Southern Comfort
¾ ounce amaretto
Splash of grenadine
Fill with half orange juice, half pineapple juice.
GLASS: Collins glass, with ice
FRUIT: cherry

Hot Buttered Rum (build)

1½ ounces rum
Fill with hot water; float butter pat.
GLASS: coffee mug
GARNISH: cinnamon stick and dash of nutmeg

Hot Toddy (build)

1½ ounce liquor
1 teaspoon sugar
Fill with boiling water.
GLASS: Old Fashioned

Hurricane (shake)

1 ounce light rum
1 ounce dark rum
¼ ounce Rose's Lime Juice
¼ ounce passion fruit syrup
GLASS: cocktail

Iced Tea
See: Long Island Iced Tea.

International Stinger (build)
Also known as Mediterranean Stinger.

1 ounce Metaxa brandy
1 ounce Galliano
GLASS: rocks, with ice

Irish Coffee (build)

1½ ounces Irish whiskey
Fill with coffee; top with whipped cream.
GLASS: coffee mug or specialty glass

Jack Rose, Cocktail (shake)

1½ ounces apple jack
1 ounce lemon mix
Splash of grenadine
GLASS: cocktail
FRUIT: cherry

Jack Rose, Highball (build)

1½ ounces apple jack
Fill with cranberry juice.
GLASS: highball, with ice

Jamaican Coffee (build)

1½ ounces Tia Maria
Fill with coffee; top with whipped cream.
GLASS: coffee mug or specialty glass

Jelly Bean (build)

1 ounce Southern Comfort
½ ounce anisette
Drop of grenadine
GLASS: shot

½ Blackberry brandy
½ anisette
OR
WHISKEY & ANISETTE

John Collins (shake)
A Tom Collins made with whiskey instead of gin.

1½ ounces whiskey
Fill with lemon mix and shake.
GLASS: Collins, with ice
FRUIT: orange and cherry

 Kamikaze (build)

1 ounce vodka
1 ounce triple sec
Few drops Rose's Lime Juice
GLASS: rocks, with ice

King Alphonse (build)

1 ounce dark crème de cacao
Float cream to brim.
GLASS: pony or pousse-café

Kioki Coffee (build)

½ ounce coffee liqueur
½ ounce dark crème de cacao
½ ounce brandy
Fill with coffee; top with whipped cream.
GLASS: coffee mug or specialty glass

Kir (build)

White wine
Splash of crème de cassis
GLASS: wine
(For history, see p. 65)

Long Island Iced Tea (shake lightly)

½ ounce vodka
½ ounce rum
½ ounce gin
½ ounce triple sec
½ ounce tequila ——— *ASK IF WANTED*
Fill with lemon mix.
Add squirt of cola.
GLASS: Collins
FRUIT: lime wedge

Madras (build)
A cran-orange Screwdriver.

1½ ounces vodka
Fill with half orange, half cranberry juice.
GLASS: highball, with ice

Mai Tai (build)

1½ ounces rum
½ ounce crème de almond (crème de noyau)
Fill with pineapple juice.
GLASS: Old Fashioned, with ice
FRUIT: pineapple stick and cherry

Manhattan (stir)

2 ounces whiskey
½ ounce sweet vermouth
GLASS: cocktail
FRUIT: cherry

Manhattan, Dry (stir)

2 ounces whiskey
½ ounce *dry* vermouth
GLASS: cocktail
FRUIT: twist

Manhattan, Perfect (stir)

2 ounces whiskey
¼ ounce sweet vermouth
¼ ounce dry vermouth
GLASS: cocktail
FRUIT: twist

Manhattan, West Coast Variation (stir)

Use bourbon instead of blended whiskey.

Margarita (shake)

1 ounce tequila
½ ounce triple sec
1 ounce lime mix
GLASS: cocktail, with salted rim
FRUIT: lime

Marilyn (build)

1½ ounces amaretto
Fill halfway with milk.
Shake, then top with 7-Up.
GLASS: Collins, with ice

Martini, Bone Dry (stir)

2½ ounces gin
GLASS: cocktail
FRUIT: olive or twist

Martini, Dry (stir)

2 ounces gin
½ ounce dry vermouth
GLASS: cocktail
FRUIT: olive
(For history, see p. 14.)

Martini, Extra Dry (stir)

2½ ounces gin
Few drops dry vermouth
GLASS: cocktail
FRUIT: olive

Mediterranean Stinger
See: International Stinger.

Melonball (build)

1 ounce Midori
1 ounce vodka
Fill with orange juice.
GLASS: Collins, with ice
FRUIT: lime and cherry

Mexican Coffee (build)

1½ ounces Kahlua
Fill with coffee; top with whipped cream.
GLASS: coffee mug or specialty glass

Mexican Screw (build)

A Screwdriver made with tequila instead of vodka

1½ ounces tequila
Fill with orange juice.
GLASS: highball, with ice

Mimosa (build)

1 part orange juice
1 part champagne
GLASS: wine
FRUIT: orange slice

Mint Julep (build)

Muddle:
    A few mint leaves
    1 teaspoon sugar
    Splash of club soda
Fill with crushed ice.
Add 2 ounces bourbon.
GLASS: Collins
GARNISH: mint leaves

Moscow Mule (build)

1½ ounces vodka
½ ounce Rose's Lime Juice
Fill with ginger beer.
GLASS: Collins, with ice
FRUIT: lime wedge

Mudslide (shake)

¾ ounce vodka
¾ ounce coffee liqueur *KAHULA*
¾ ounce Irish cream liqueur
GLASS: rocks, with ice

Mulled Cider

1 quart cider
6 whole cloves
Grated nutmeg

Heat without boiling and serve in mugs.
Add 1½ ounces rum, or cognac, or—best of all—Calvados to
  each mug

Negroni (stir)

1 ounce gin
1 ounce Campari
½ ounce sweet vermouth
GLASS: cocktail
FRUIT: twist

Old Fashioned (build)

Into an Old Fashioned glass (slightly larger than a rocks
  glass) put:
  An orange slice and a cherry
  1 teaspoon of sugar
  Few dashes of Angostura bitters
  Splash of club soda
Muddle (stir the ingredients while squashing the fruit) with
  a pestle or, if this is not available, a bar spoon.
Fill the glass with ice.
Add 1½ ounces whiskey.
Put a splash of club soda on top.
(The fruit is sometimes added last, and not muddled. The
  final splash of soda is sometimes omitted.)

Orange Blossom (stir)

1½ ounces gin
1 ounce orange juice
GLASS: cocktail

Pearl Harbor (build)

1 ounce Midori
1 ounce rum
Fill with pineapple juice.
GLASS: Collins, with ice
FRUIT: lime and cherry

Peppermint Patty (build)

1 ounce peppermint schnapps
1 ounce dark crème de cacao
GLASS: rocks, with ice

Pimm's Cup (build)

There are five Pimm's Cups—Number 1 seems the most popular

1½ ounces Pimm's Cup
Fill with 7-Up.
GLASS: highball, with ice
FRUIT: twist

Pina Colada (blend)

2 ounces rum
1 tablespoon coconut syrup
Pineapple juice
Ice
GLASS: brandy snifter or specialty glass
GARNISH: pineapple stick or, if not available, cherry

Pink Gin (stir)

2½ ounces gin
Dash of Angostura bitters
GLASS: cocktail

Pink Lady (shake)

1 ounce gin
1 ounce cream (or milk)
½ ounce grenadine
GLASS: champagne

Pink Squirrel (shake)

1 ounce crème de almond (crème de noyau)
½ ounce white crème de cacao
1 ounce cream (or milk)
GLASS: champagne

Pisco Sour (shake)

1½ ounces Pisco brandy
½ ounce lemon mix
½ egg white
Dash of Angostura bitters
GLASS: cocktail, with sugared rim
GARNISH: orange and cherry

Planter's Punch (build)

1 ounce rum
½ ounce apricot brandy
½ ounce triple sec

Splash grenadine
Fill with half and half grapefruit and orange juice.
GLASS: Collins, with ice
FRUIT: orange slice

Port Cocktail (stir)

2½ ounces port
1 tablespoon brandy
GLASS: cocktail

Pousse Café (build)
Pronounced "poose caffay."

If poured carefully over the back of a spoon, liquors of
    different densities will remain in separate layers in the
    glass. If these layers are also of contrasting colors, the
    effect can be very showy, like a liquid rainbow.
All Pousse Café recipes, including the ones below, need to
    be pretested before using. The reason for this is that the
    density of a liqueur will often vary from one
    manufacturer to another, depending on the proof and the
    amount of sugar used. One brand may have an orange
    curaçao that floats cleanly on top of the crème de
    menthe of the same brand. The same two liqueurs made
    by another manufacturer, however, may blend together
    in a muddy mess.
So use the recipes given here as a starting point only and
    discover by trial and error, or by asking a more
    experienced bartender, what can be done with the liquors
    available in the bar where you are working.
Pour in the order given.
(See also: B-52, Champerelle, King Alphonse)

Pousse Café No. 1

1 part crème de bananes
1 part Cherry Heering
1 part cognac

Pousse Café No. 2

1 part maraschino liqueur
1 part crème de violette
1 part Green Chartreuse
1 part cognac

Pousse Café No. 3

1 part light crème de cacao
1 part cherry liqueur
1 part Kummel
1 part cream

Pousse Café No. 4

1 part maraschino liqueur
1 part green crème de menthe
1 part Yellow Chartreuse
1 part orange curaçao
1 part cognac

Pousse Café No. 5

1 part maraschino liqueur
1 part orange curaçao
1 part Green Chartreuse
1 part anisette
1 part cognac

Pousse Café No. 6

1 part anisette
1 part Parfait Amour
1 part Yellow Chartreuse
1 part Green Chartreuse
1 part orange curaçao
1 part cognac

Pousse Café No. 7

1 part grenadine
1 part Yellow Chartreuse
1 part crème d'yvette
1 part white crème de menthe
1 part Green Chartreuse
1 part cognac

Prairie Fire (build)

1½ ounces tequila
Tabasco sauce to taste
GLASS: rocks, with ice

Prairie Oyster (blend)

A folk medicine hangover prescription.

1 egg
1 teaspoon worcestershire sauce

1 teaspoon catsup
½ teaspoon vinegar
Salt and pepper
Dash of tabasco
Small scoop of ice
GLASS: champagne

Purple Jesus (build)

1½ ounces vodka
Grape juice to fill
GLASS: highball, with ice

Ramos Fizz (shake)

2 ounces gin
2 ounces lemon mix
1 egg white
1 tablespoon cream
½ teaspoon orange flower water
Shake with ice and strain into highball glass with just a
    few ice cubes.
Fill with club soda.

Red Suspenders

*A glass of beer with a skosh of tomato juice, sometimes served
    with a salt shaker.*

Rob Roy (stir)

A Manhattan made with scotch instead of blended whiskey.

2 ounces scotch
½ ounce sweet vermouth
GLASS: cocktail
FRUIT: cherry

Rusty Nail (build)

1½ ounces scotch
½ ounce Drambuie
GLASS: rocks, with ice

Rye Presbyterian, or "Rye Pres" (build)

1½ ounces whiskey
Fill with half club soda, half ginger ale.
GLASS: highball, with ice

Salty Dog (build)
A greyhound with a salted rim.

1½ ounces vodka
Grapefruit juice to fill
GLASS: highball, with ice

Sangria

4 ounces red wine
½ ounce lemon mix
½ ounce orange juice
Club soda to fill
GLASS: snifter, with ice

Sazerac (build)

1 ounce anisette
1 ounce rum
Dash Angostura bitters
Dash orange bitters
Club soda to fill
GLASS: Collins, with ice
FRUIT: twist

Scotch Mist (build)

1½ ounces scotch
GLASS: rocks, with crushed ice
FRUIT: twist

Screwdriver (build)

1½ ounces vodka
Orange juice to fill
GLASS: highball, with ice

Seabreeze (build)

1½ ounces vodka
Fill with half grapefruit, half cranberry juice.
GLASS: highball, with ice

*bay breeze –
w/ pineapple & cranberry*

Shandy Gaff (build)

1 part beer
1 part ginger ale
GLASS: Collins

Shirley Temple (build)

Splash of grenadine in a glass of ginger ale
GLASS: Old Fashioned, with ice
FRUIT: two cherries

Sicilian Kiss (build)

1 ounce amaretto
1 ounce Southern Comfort
GLASS: rocks, with ice

Side Car (shake)
*A Margarita made with brandy instead of tequila, and without the
    salt.*

1 ounce brandy
½ ounce triple sec
1 ounce lemon mix
GLASS: cocktail

Silver Bullet (build)

1 ounce tequila
1 ounce peppermint schnapps
GLASS: rocks, with ice

 Singapore Sling (shake)

1 ounce gin
½ ounce sloe gin
½ ounce cherry brandy
Fill with lemon mix and shake.
GLASS: Collins, with ice
FRUIT: cherry
(For history, see p. 81)

Sloe Comfortable Screw (build)

1 ounce sloe gin
1 ounce Southern Comfort
Orange juice to fill
GLASS: Collins, with ice

Sloe Comfortable Screw Against the Wall (build)

1 ounce sloe gin
1 ounce Southern Comfort
Orange juice to fill
½ ounce Galliano to float on top
GLASS: Collins, with ice

Sloe Gin Fizz (shake)

1½ ounces sloe gin
Fill almost all the way with lemon mix.
Shake, then top up with club soda.
GLASS: Collins, with ice
FRUIT: cherry

Sloe Screw (build)
A Screwdriver made with sloe gin instead of vodka.

1½ ounces sloe gin
Orange juice to fill
GLASS: highball, with ice

Snake Bite (build)

1½ ounces Yukon Jack
½ ounce Rose's Lime Juice
GLASS: rocks, with ice

Sombrero (shake)

1½ ounces coffee liqueur
Fill with milk and shake.
GLASS: highball, with ice
(Sometimes also served in a rocks glass, with just a
    splash of milk or cream.)

Stinger (stir)˙

1½ ounces brandy
1 ounce white crème de menthe
GLASS: cocktail

Tequila Sunrise (build)

1½ ounces tequila
Splash of grenadine
Orange juice to fill
GLASS: Collins, with ice
FRUIT: orange slice

Tequila Sunset (build)

1½ ounces tequila
Orange juice to fill
½ ounce blackberry brandy to float
GLASS: highball, with ice

Toasted Almond (build)

1 ounce coffee liqueur
1 ounce amaretto
Fill with milk and shake.
(Sometimes also served in a rocks glass, with just a splash of
    milk or cream.)

Tom Collins (shake)

1½ ounces gin
Fill with lemon mix and shake.
GLASS: Collins, with ice
FRUIT: orange and cherry
(For history, see p. 18)

Tuesday Weld (shake)

¾ ounce brandy
¾ ounce dark crème de cacao
1 ounce cream (or milk)
GLASS: cocktail
GARNISH: Oreo cookie

Universal 92 (build)

¾ ounce vodka
¾ ounce amaretto
¾ ounce Midori
Pineapple juice to fill
GLASS: Collins, with ice
FRUIT: lime and cherry

Universe (build)

1 ounce vodka
½ ounce Midori
½ ounce pistachio liqueur
Pineapple juice to fill
GLASS: Collins, with ice
FRUIT: lime and cherry

Velvet Hammer (shake)
A Rusty Nail with cream.

1½ ounces scotch
½ ounce Drambuie
Splash of cream
GLASS: rocks, with ice

Velvet Hammer No. 2 (shake)

¾ ounce vodka
¾ ounce dark crème de cacao
1 ounce cream (or milk)
GLASS: cocktail

Velvet Hammer No. 3 (shake)

1 ounce Strega
1 ounce white crème de cacao
½ ounce cream (or milk)
GLASS: cocktail

Vermouth Cassis (build)

1½ ounces dry vermouth
½ ounce crème de cassis
GLASS: rocks
FRUIT: twist

Virgin Mary (shake)
A Bloody Mary with no alcohol.

½ ounce Rose's Lime Juice
4 dashes worcestershire sauce
1 dash tabasco
Salt and pepper
Fill with tomato juice and shake lightly.
GLASS: Collins, with ice
FRUIT: celery stalk

Vodka Collins (shake)

1½ ounces vodka
Fill with lemon mix and shake.
GLASS: Collins, with ice
FRUIT: orange and cherry

Ward 8 (shake)
A tall Whiskey Sour with a splash of grenadine.

1½ ounces whiskey
Splash of grenadine
Fill with lemon mix and shake.
GLASS: Collins, with ice
FRUIT: orange and cherry

Warsaw (shake)

1 ounce vodka
1 ounce blackberry brandy
¼ ounce dry vermouth
¼ ounce lemon mix
GLASS: cocktail

Whiskey Sour (shake)

1½ ounces whiskey
1 ounce lemon mix
GLASS: sour
FRUIT: orange and cherry

White Russian (shake)

1 ounce coffee liqueur
1 ounce vodka
Fill with milk and shake.
GLASS: Collins, with ice
(Sometimes also served in a rocks glass, with just a splash of
    milk or cream.)

Wine Cooler (build)

Two-thirds wine, one-third 7-Up in a Collins glass, with ice.

Wine Spritzer (build)

*Two-thirds wine, usually white, and one-third club soda in a
    Collins glass, with ice.*

Zippy (shake)

1 ounce dark crème de cacao
1 ounce Irish cream liqueur
Tabasco to taste
GLASS: rocks, with ice

Zombie (shake or blend)
Remember: 3 rums, 3 juices, 3 sweeteners.

1 ounce light rum
1 ounce dark rum
½ ounce orange curaçao
½ ounce apricot brandy
½ ounce Rose's Lime Juice
½ ounce papaya juice
Fill with half pineapple, half grapefruit juice.
Float 1 ounce 151° rum.
GLASS: ceramic skull mug
FRUIT: pineapple stick and sprig of mint

For Further Reading

Mr. Boston Deluxe Official Bartender's Guide. Boston: Mr. Boston Distiller Corporation, 1978. Mr. Boston always seems at least ten years behind the times, and contains many very obscure drinks, but it is still very useful for general reference.

Trader Vic's Bartender's Guide, by Trader Vic. New York: Doubleday, 1972. This is not quite as well organized for quick reference as Mr. Boston, but Trader Vic's special recipes for his own chain of restaurants have a complexity and subtlety not found elsewhere.

Notes on a Cellar Book, by George Saintsbury. New York: W. H. Smith Publishers, 1978. A witty and erudite essay on his wine cellar—which also contained stronger spirits—by an eminent Victorian souse.

Under the Influence: A Guide to the Myths and Realities of Alcoholism, by James R. Milam and Katherine Ketcham. Seattle: Madrona Publishers, 1981. A carefully researched study of our perceptions of alcoholism, and of its causes—which are thought to be largely genetic and biochemical—and of the possibilities for treatment.

The Bon Vivant's Companion, or, How to Mix Drinks, by Professor Jerry Thomas, ed. Herbert Asbury. New York: Grosset and Dunlap, 1934. A bartender's guide from a century ago, written by the creator of the Martini.

Buller's Bar Exam

1. "Straight up" means
   a. a drink served in a tall glass.
   b. a drink made with straight liquor.
   c. a drink that is chilled, but served without ice.
   d. a drink that is swallowed with one gulp.

2. A "bone dry" Martini is
   a. a Martini made with very little vermouth.
   b. a Martini made with no vermouth.
   c. a Martini made with very little gin.
   d. a Martini made with very little ice.

3. A "perfect" Manhattan is
   a. a Manhattan made with half sweet and half dry vermouth.
   b. a Manhattan made with no vermouth.
   c. a Manhattan served with two cherries.
   d. a Manhattan made with bourbon.

4. A Manhattan (straight up) is
   a. a shake drink.
   b. a build drink.
   c. a stir drink.
   d. a blender drink.

5. A Screwdriver is
   a. a shake drink.
   b. a build drink.
   c. a stir drink.
   d. a blender drink.

6. A Daiquiri is
   a. a shake drink.
   b. a build drink.
   c. a stir drink.
   d. a blender drink.

7. The common ingredient of the Screwdriver, the Bloody Mary, the Black Russian, and the Madras is
   a. vodka.
   b. orange juice.
   c. coffee liqueur.
   d. grapefruit juice.

8. The ingredients of a Harvey Wallbanger are vodka, orange juice, and
   a. triple sec.
   b. amaretto.
   c. Galliano.
   d. Rose's Lime Juice.

9. A Gibson is
   a. a Manhattan served with an olive instead of a cherry.
   b. a Martini served with a cocktail onion instead of an olive.
   c. a Gimlet served with a cherry instead of a lime wedge.
   d. a Rob Roy served with a lime instead of a cherry.

10. Gin and Tonic, Rum and Coke, and Scotch and Soda are all
    a. top shelf drinks.
    b. stir drinks.
    c. rocks drinks.
    d. highballs.

11. If a customer orders "Scotch and Soda," you should give him
    or her
    a. bar scotch.
    b. call-brand scotch.
    c. top shelf scotch.
    d. domestic scotch.

12. Drinks with tonic
    a. should never be served with ice.
    b. should always be served with a piece of lime.
    c. should never include rum.
    d. are always top shelf drinks.

13. A "twist" is
    a. a drink that has been lightly stirred.
    b. a piece of lime.
    c. a few drops of tabasco sauce.
    d. a piece of lemon peel.

14. The proper garnish for a Bloody Mary is
    a. a cherry.
    b. a plum tomato.
    c. a celery stalk.
    d. a plum tomato.

15. The proper garnish for a Brandy Alexander is
    a. grated nutmeg.
    b. whipped cream.
    c. a cherry.
    d. an orange slice.

16. The head on a glass of beer may collapse if
    a. the beer is too warm.
    b. the pressure from the keg is too high.
    c. the beer has too much salt.
    d. the glass has a trace of grease in it.

17. Most American beers are
    a. ales.
    b. lagers.
    c. stouts.
    d. malt liquors.

18. The proper temperature for serving red wine is
    a. 36–45° F.
    b. 45–50° F.
    c. 50–55° F.
    d. room temperature.

19. A 100 proof liquor contains
    a. 50 percent alcohol.
    b. 100 percent alcohol.
    c. 86 percent alcohol.
    d. 10 percent alcohol.

20. Brandy is made from
    a. bran.
    b. soybeans.
    c. wine.
    d. kerosene.

21. The predominant flavor in Kahlua is
    a. tequila.
    b. coffee.
    c. herbs and spices.
    d. orange peel.

22. In most states, a person is guilty of drunk driving if his or her blood alcohol level is more than
    a. one percent.
    b. ten percent.
    c. one-tenth of one percent.
    d. three-tenths of one percent.

23. A Pine Float is
    a. a Pina Colada with a scoop of ice cream.
    b. vodka on the rocks, with a splash of pineapple juice.
    c. pineapple juice served with a cherry.
    d. a toothpick in a glass of water.

24. John Collins was
    a. an English waiter.
    b. a Scottish brewer.
    c. a California bartender.
    d. a Long Island stereo salesman.

25. Bitters and Soda is
    a. a remedy for hiccups.
    b. a remedy for an upset stomach.
    c. a remedy for headache
    d. an effective stain remover.

ANSWERS TO FINAL EXAM

1. c.	6. a.	11. a.	16. d.	21. b.
2. b.	7. a.	12. b.	17. b.	22. c.
3. a.	8. c.	13. d.	18. d.	23. d.
4. c.	9. b.	14. c.	19. a.	24. a.
5. b.	10. d.	15. a.	20. c.	25. b.

If you got any wrong, look up the answers. If you got more than ten wrong, you should read through the course again.

DIPLOMA

Be it known that _____, upon the successful
completion of Buller's Professional Course in Bartending,
should be eminently qualified to practice professional

MIXOLOGY

either full time or part time, for amusement or profit.

Jon Buller

JON BULLER
PROFESSOR OF ETHYL PHARMACOLOGY

Index

FEEDBACK REQUESTED

For use in future editions, I'd like to hear from readers with new recipes, bartender jokes, real-life anecdotes, hiccups remedies, or any other suggestions and corrections. If your contribution is used, you will receive a free copy of the next edition, with my thanks.

Jon Buller
c/o The Harvard Common Press
535 Albany Street
Boston, Massachusetts 02118